MUNCHIES
Guide to Dinner

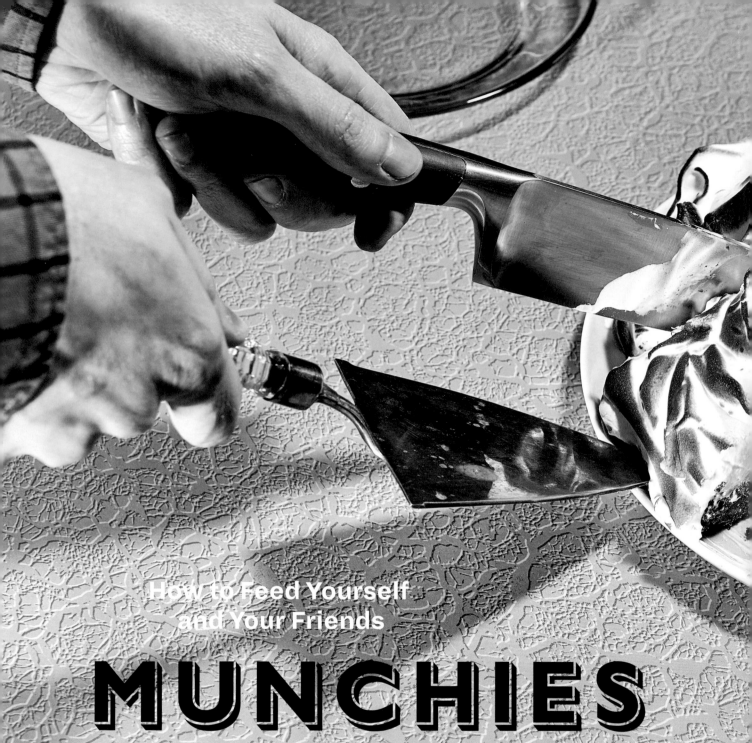

How to Feed Yourself
and Your Friends

MUNCHIES
Guide to Dinner

Editors of **MUNCHIES**

photography by Heami Lee
recipes by Farideh Sadeghin

TEN SPEED PRESS
California | New York

CONTENTS

INTRODUCTION

In the time MUNCHIES has been around, we've gotten to work with all kinds of chefs, making food that ranges from lowbrow to highbrow and everywhere in between. Add to that the fact that almost all of us have spent serious time in kitchens ourselves and have super-high expectations of what food should be, what you get is a team of people who are pretty damn good at parsing pro-level skills and techniques into very tasty home-cook–friendly food.

This book is a culmination of all those skills: in short, this is how we cook when we're at home. Most of the time, because we're people with jobs and lives, we're putting together quick dinners that keep us fed and happy. But we really love food and love feeding people and don't think there's a better way to enjoy the company of others than around a giant table of food. So, to that end, welcome to the *MUNCHIES Guide to Dinner*, our effort to turn the way we like to cook and eat into a collection of recipes. Easy ones for busy weeknights, and fancy ones for the occasional weekend dinner parties with friends.

We've divided the recipes in here into four sections: Homemade Staples, Essentials, Weeknight Meals, and Weekend Entertaining.

Homemade Staples is where we offer primers on all the things that add so much character to your meals if you make them yourself: recipes like homemade mayo and salad dressings, chicken stock, tomato sauce, and fresh pasta from scratch for the days you're feeling ambitious. Do you have to make them at home? No. Will they kick ass if you do? Yes.

Essentials are the techniques and dishes we think everyone should know—the ones that maybe your parents would have taught you if you lived inside a Norman Rockwell painting, where you don't really want to admit, "Uh, shit, I can't believe I don't know how to do this": the roast chickens, the mashed potatoes, the pots of plain rice. With these basics, you can build all the elements and flavors you need to keep yourself fed and happy. They might not all be the quickest and easiest—although some are, for sure—but they're exactly what you'll want to have in your arsenal when a mac-and-cheese emergency comes along.

Weeknight Meals are exactly what they sound like: they're what you fix yourself after a long day at work or school. They don't generally require a lot of complicated shopping or prep, and for the most part, they'll get you dinner on the table in under an hour. There are also a couple of recipes in that section (the Chicken Pot Pie on page 105, for example) that work perfectly if you make them on a weekend and freeze your leftovers in batches. Then you'll have a very easy pop-it-in-the-oven-and-crack-a-beer-while-you-wait situation when you get home on a Tuesday evening.

Weekend Entertaining is loosely organized theme nights for when you want to invite your friends over and go all out. They're intended as inspiration; no one's saying Pimento Cheese Quesadillas and Cacio e Pepe Popcorn are mandatory for a Netflix binge-watching party (see page 113) . . . but no one's saying they're not, either. Treat these as loose suggestions, or shoot a couple of recipes over to each of your friends and make it a potluck.

We really want you to treat everything in here as a suggestion. We have thoughts and opinions about what goes with what, and how best to use leftovers, but fundamentally, the point of this book is to give you the knowledge base and skill set you need to be comfortable improvising on your own. We're hoping this book gives you the tools and skills you need to make yourself (and your friends and loved ones) many, many dinners that live up to your deservedly high expectations.

What You'll Need to Have on Hand

The recommended pantry for *MUNCHIES Guide to Dinner* probably isn't all that different from what you already have at home. You'll want some staples: flour, unsalted butter, white and brown sugar, eggs, kosher salt, oils (olive oil and something heat-friendly like canola or grapeseed) and black pepper (whole peppercorns in a pepper grinder, please). Buy spices from the sort of store that has frequent turnover, in small quantities, and keep them somewhere cool and dark (like not right on top of the stove). If your oils are ancient, they're probably not good anymore—a handy test is that if the oil smells like a basement, odds are it's rancid and you should toss it (pour it into the garbage, not down the drain) and get new oil.

Most dishes here can be made with ingredients from your average urban supermarket. If a recipe calls for specific things, like semolina flour or toban djan, that you can't find locally, you can always find them either online—at everyone's favorite large conglomerate or a smaller purveyor—or at a specialty shop (and we promise we call for fancy shit only when it's absolutely necessary).

A couple of quick notes about grocery shopping: it takes a little practice, but with time it's not hard to shop like a pro.

Buy only as much as you think you need or will finish before it goes bad. And with that in mind, don't be afraid of the idea of precut or prepackaged produce. Are you shopping just for yourself? Odds are you're not going to be able to finish a whole eight-pound watermelon. Buy the quartered section that's wrapped in plastic wrap, and you'll end up not throwing away as much of your money in the form of food waste. (If you're morally opposed to single-use plastics, then you'd better really love watermelon.) Same with things like onions. If you're shopping for just yourself, a single onion (as opposed to the five-pound bag) might make more sense for you, and the price difference per unit is negligible.

If your local grocery store uses water misters to keep the produce looking shiny and fresh, try to pick the pieces that are farther back on the shelf or on the bottom of the pile where the water doesn't reach. Wet produce, especially if it's not stored properly, will rot much faster. Also, the older produce is moved to the top of the pile when the store restocks the shelves, so the freshest stuff is on the bottom anyway.

And please don't be afraid of the butcher or fishmonger. Sure, we live in an age where we don't have to take a ticket, get in line, and wait to be called by a big burly butcher in a blood-stained apron to order our preferred cuts of beef by weight. Most of the proteins we buy are sold in limited-weight packages on plastic-wrapped Styrofoam trays, so we can pick them up without ever having to speak to another human if we don't want to. But you should still get to know the person behind the counter! Even in a big chain grocery store, they can be super-helpful if you don't know the difference between a hanger and a skirt steak, or what the hell to do with chicken necks. And if you go to an actual butcher or fishmonger, the difference in the quality of both product and service you'll get is night and day, so it's kind of a no-brainer.

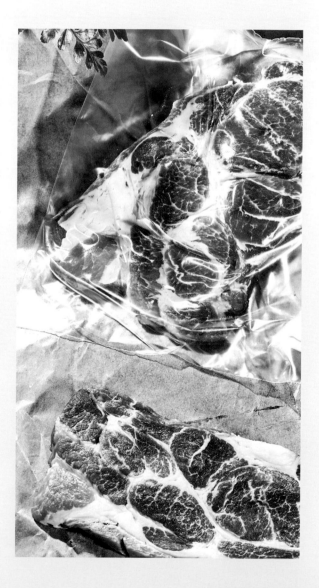

The Equipment You'll Need

You don't need a ton of tools to set up a working kitchen. Really, a couple of decent knives, a cutting board, a cast-iron skillet, assorted saucepans, a couple of sheet pans, and large pot and colander for cooking pasta should get you through most of the recipes in this book. But if you've got the cash, here's the full lot of equipment that we recommend you stock up on.

Knives

A chef's knife (as big as you can comfortably handle; we like an 8-inch to 10-inch blade), a paring knife, and a long serrated knife. Skip the box sets; they somehow manage to be both more and less than you need at the same time.

Pans

Get a skillet with an oven-safe handle (that means metal or some kind of super futuristic silicone-esque alloy, but tbh, that means metal). Would be nice if that skillet had a lid, too. A little nonstick guy would be good for eggs, and you'll also definitely want a cast-iron skillet. You've probably heard a bunch of things about how you can never wash a cast-iron skillet, and how it'll be ruined if you look at it the wrong way or whatever. These are all lies. Yes, cast-iron pans do require seasoning–even the ones that come seasoned already. If you're buying a brand-new pan, you should wash it well, then dry it carefully and rub it all over with a thin film of vegetable oil. Put it upside down on the rack in a 350°F oven (put a baking sheet on the rack below it to catch drips) and let it hang out in the oven for about an hour. And then you're good. (Just use a kitchen towel to take it out of there.) You can use soap when you wash it, just oil it lightly afterwards. It's true that you shouldn't go to town scrubbing it with steel wool, because you don't want to rub off all of your hard-earned seasoning, but you also don't want a pan smelling of rancid fat sitting on your stove all the time, either. If you manage to really get something stuck on there, heat it up on the stove and add some water to deglaze it; it should come unstuck easily enough.

Pots

Something big enough in which to cook long pasta and make stock (like an 8-quart enameled pot), then maybe a 2-quart pot with a lid for melting butter and cooking rice. You'll also benefit from—and this is something to save up for—a 6-quart cast-iron Dutch oven, which will be your go-to for braising and big batches.

Utensils

You'll want some rubber spatulas, a whisk, a ladle, a couple of wooden spoons, some lockable metal tongs, a can opener, a vegetable peeler, a box grater, and a microplane. Don't forget to have a set each of measuring cups and spoons on hand, too. Everything listed here should be cheap, so no need to go crazy. If you do a bunch of deep-frying, you'll want a spider, which is a slotted wire spoon that's great for scooping things out of hot oil. A digital instant-read thermometer isn't a bad idea, either; it will come in handy if you're going to be cooking meat. Get a potato masher if mashed potatoes = life for you.

Sheet Pans

They're good for baking, obviously, but also for roasting vegetables; the pizza on page 157; putting under cobblers and pies and lasagnas so nothing bubbles onto the oven floor and smokes out your kitchen; corralling ingredients when you're making something complicated; and probably a bunch of other things we're forgetting. They're also cheap as hell. Get a couple of half-sheet and a couple of quarter-sheet pans. If you have an oven big enough to fit a full-size sheet at home you're probably much too fancy for this book, but also, we'll be right over.

Cutting Boards and Mixing Bowls

Don't get a glass cutting board (it messes up your knives). The fancy heavy wooden ones look cool, and you can serve finished food on them, too, but they can be expensive. Plastic is just fine. As far as bowls go, a bunch of nesting ones are easy to store; stainless steel from a restaurant supply store is probably cheapest, but if being able to microwave food in your bowl is important to you, go with plastic or glass.

Hand Mixer

So, you don't necessarily need a hand mixer, but whipping things like egg whites by hand can be a real drag. A decent hand mixer is usually $20 to $30, and takes up way less space than a stand mixer. Use your mixer to get stiff peaks for Meringue Cookies (page 72) and to cream butter for your Cast-Iron Cookie Sundae (page 127).

Food Processor

You definitely don't need this, but there are a couple of things a food processor really excels at: making pesto (page 34), hummus, homemade breadcrumbs, and helping things like the home-made mayo (page 24) emulsify.

How to Cook Safely

According to the FDA, over forty-eight million people get food poisoning in the United States every year. Of those cases, the Center for Science in the Public Interest estimates that well over a third come from home-cooked foods rather than restaurant food. Don't be another statistic! If you're the kind of person who likes to play fast and loose with cleanliness in your apartment (if you haven't washed your bedsheets in two months, we're talking to you), familiarize yourself with some of the most basic basics of at-home food safety. From how to not cross-contaminate your raw veggies with potential E. coli from your raw steak, to how to know when it's really time to throw out that carton of eggs, here are some rules of thumb for how to keep your food safe and save you money. (Because the more you throw away, the more cash you're throwing away, too.)

Use a separate, plastic cutting board for raw meats and fish, and clean it well when you're done. Cross-contamination from raw meats is an easy way to end up with a surprise case of food poisoning, so spring for one extra piece of kitchen equipment for the sake of safety.

Wash your freaking hands, you goblin. More often than you think you should. Rubbed your sweaty face while chopping veggies? Probs best to wash your hands. Touched raw meat? Definitely wash your hands before touching any other ingredients or your cooking utensils again. This is not rocket science; there's a good reason you've been told this since you were a little kid.

Don't rinse raw meat under water. This only serves to spread the potential for contamination all over your sink, which you probably won't remember to scrub down after you're done cooking. If your recipe calls for raw animal proteins, pat them dry with paper towels, then throw those towels away.

The fridge should be kept at a consistent 40°F or below, and the freezer a steady 0°F. If you're unsure about the temperature of your fridge, pick up a thermometer from a hardware store, let it hang out in there for a day, and check on it every few hours to see if the temperature is fluctuating wildly or if it's consistently at a safe level.

The longer it takes for food to cool down in the fridge, the greater the chance for bacteria to take hold. If you're putting something into the fridge that is still hot, spread it out evenly on a sheet pan to let everything come down to a safe temperature quickly. The danger zone in which hot food has the potential to grow bacteria is between 40°F and 140°F, so the faster you get your food under 40°F, the better. If you're putting hot soup, for instance, into the fridge, put it in a wide, shallow pan or plastic container; the larger surface area will help cool it down faster. Then transfer the contents to a smaller storage container if necessary. In general, your food should go from 140°F to 70°F in two hours, then down to 41°F or cooler within four hours of reaching 70°F. Letting something cool on the counter, especially if it's hot in your kitchen, might not be enough.

Store dairy products in the rear of the fridge, where it's more consistently cold. It might be easier to get to your milk carton if you keep it in the door, but that is typically the warmest part of the refrigerator, because the temperature fluctuates as you open and close the door.

Store your raw meats or fish on the bottom shelf of your fridge, well wrapped. If by some chance any liquid leaks out, it won't drip or come into contact with other raw foods or containers.

Chicken (stand-alone thighs or breasts) should be cooked to an internal temperature of 165°F. If you're roasting a whole chicken or, say, a turkey for the holidays, the whole bird should reach 165°F. Insert a thermometer into the thickest part of the thigh, as close to the bone as possible.

Beef should be cooked to a minimum of 145°F, which is medium. Which is why menus advise that "raw or undercooked" beef can cause food-borne illnesses. (BTW 125°F is rare and 135°F is medium-rare, but we didn't tell you that.)

Pork should be cooked to 160°F. (Trichinosis, however, dies at 145°F.)

Eggs will keep for five weeks in the fridge at a constant temperature. The sell-by date on the packaging will likely be sooner than that five-week window, so mark the actual expiration date on the carton with a Sharpie if you think you might forget. If you've cracked an egg open and are only using either the whites or the yolks and saving the unused part, don't keep it more than two or three days in an airtight container. Freeze leftover whites in a tightly sealed container for up to three months.

Fish should not smell fishy when you unwrap it. A fishmonger's general rule of thumb is that if it still smells like the ocean, it's fresh. Whether lean or fatty, raw fish is really safe only for up to two days.

Canned goods should be free from dents and bulges. Check the cans before you leave the store; these are an indication that the seal on the can might have been compromised, and the risk of bacteria starting to grow and create botulism inside is increased. If a can on your shelf is showing signs of bulging, it's time to toss it, as that's another sign of botulism.

Store flours or grains in airtight containers for up to a year. If you're using fresh-milled flour, with the germ from the wheat still in the mix, you'll have to keep it in the fridge or freezer, and it will hold for only a few months. (Although if you're the kind of person who chooses to buy and bake with fresh-milled flour, you probably already know this.) The most common sign of flour or grains going bad is the presence of flour bugs, which look like teensy weensy brown beetles. If it smells rancid, which is an indication that too much moisture got into your storage container, it's time to toss it. If you use whole-wheat flour, just know that its shelf life is significantly shorter than white all-purpose flour, so check on it more often.

Raw meat can go bad in the fridge. As soon as raw beef or pork or any other protein is processed in a meat grinder, there is an infinite number of new nooks, crannies, and air pockets in which bacteria can live and start to wreak havoc. Keep ground meats in the fridge for only a day or two, and if you don't plan to cook them immediately, freeze them. Graying ground beef doesn't necessarily mean it's bad, but if it's gray and smells funky, it's past its prime. Whole pieces of raw meat can keep in the fridge for up to five days, but raw poultry is good for only two days. Cooked meats and poultry will keep, when properly cooled and stored, for up to four days.

Wash and replace cloth kitchen towels regularly, and make sure they have a proper chance to dry between uses. (Don't leave them crumpled up on the counter—lay them flat or hang where air can flow freely around them.)

Replace your sponge at least once a month, if not more frequently than that. If you're really concerned about daily germ accumulation and prefer to extend the life of what is essentially a single-use plastic, you can microwave a well-rinsed sponge or run it through the dishwasher on a heated dry setting to kill some germs.

Clean your counters regularly, and be sure to get the whole surface, not just the area you think you were working in. Odds are things have splashed and sprayed in a radius around your cutting board that you haven't been paying attention to. Corners and tile grout can collect some nasty stuff over time, too.

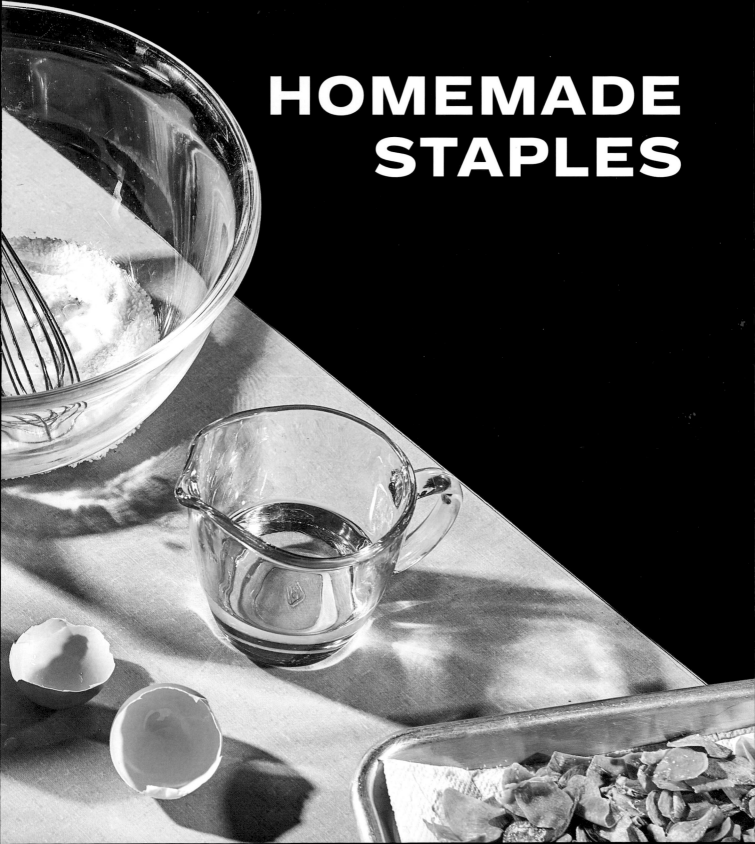

HOMEMADE STAPLES

Crispy Garlic

These crispy bits of umami goodness make everything they touch better (except maybe dessert, but watch us be proven wrong on that one). They're especially delightful on mushy things that could use a little bit of texture, like mashed potatoes (see page 62), or congee (see page 85), or roasted veggies. You can buy them in Asian markets if you don't feel like making them—but if you do make them, then you'll have the leftover, super-flavorful frying oil to add to salad dressings.

MAKES ½ CUP

2 cups vegetable oil
10 garlic cloves, peeled and thinly sliced

Pour the oil into a small saucepan over medium heat. Line a plate with paper towels. Add the garlic to the oil and cook, stirring occasionally, until the garlic starts to brown and crisp, about 9 minutes. This takes time, but once it gets going, it turns brown fast, so pay attention! As soon as it starts to turn golden, skim with a fine-mesh strainer or spider, saving the oil. Transfer the garlic chips to the paper towel–lined plate. Let the oil cool, strain it into an air-tight container, and keep it in a cool, dry place. The leftover oil is excellent for salad dressings and frying savory things. Garlic will keep in an airtight container at room temperature for up to 3 months.

Crispy Shallots

Same principle as the garlic (page 18), just shallots this time. These are good everywhere garlic is, which is to say, everywhere. Danish people even use them to top hot dogs, and who are we to argue with the Danes?

MAKES 1¼ CUPS

2 cups vegetable oil
4 shallots, peeled and thinly sliced

Pour the oil into a small saucepan over medium heat. Line a plate with paper towels. Add the shallots to the oil and cook, stirring occasionally, until the shallots start to brown and crisp, 12 minutes. This takes time, but once they get going, they turn brown fast! As soon as they start to turn golden, skim with a fine-mesh strainer or spider, saving the oil. Transfer the shallots to the paper towel–lined plate. Let the oil cool, strain it into an airtight container, and keep it in a cool, dry place. The leftover oil is excellent for salad dressings and frying savory things. Shallots will keep in an airtight container at room temperature for up to 3 months.

Quick Jalapeño Pickles

Pickling sounds way more complicated than it actually is, and it's easy to be intimidated instead of inspired by all those picturesque Pinterest tableaus of Mason jars. But fundamentally, pickling is just pouring hot vinegar over vegetables, letting them steep, and refrigerating. That's it.

If you get super into pickling, you'll want to learn about how to can vegetables safely. (Pickling for stable shelf storage is a very different process than what we're doing here, and if that's a thing you want to do, you'll need some more sophisticated equipment and protocols than the following.) That said, anything you pickle with this brine will be good for up to a week in the fridge. Pour the brine over whatever you'd like: green beans, jalapeños, radishes, okra, or, you know, cucumbers. Add whole spices like coriander seeds, black peppercorns, mustard seeds, allspice, or cinnamon sticks (toast them in a dry skillet over low heat first) or fresh herbs like dill, parsley, or mint to change up the flavor. You can use a splash of the brine to brighten up mayo-based salads or slow-cooked soups or stews.

8 whole jalapeños
1 cup white vinegar
¼ cup granulated sugar
1 tablespoon kosher salt

Pack the jalapeños into a 16-ounce Mason jar. Bring the vinegar and 1 cup water to a boil in a medium saucepan. Mix in the sugar and salt and stir until dissolved, then pour the brine over the jalapeños. Seal and refrigerate for 1 week before using.

Homemade Mayo

We're not saying you should be making every condiment at home. Fuck that. For instance, you should absolutely be buying ketchup—you won't make it better than Heinz does, tbh. But mayo? It really is just better when you DIY, and besides, you never know when you're going to be stuck at home in a snowstorm without a bottle of Hellmann's or Duke's.

Pro tip: If your mayo turns into a lumpy mess of oil and bits, add a very small splash of warm water to a clean bowl and, whisking aggressively and constantly, add the lumpy mess slowly, drop by drop, to the water. It should re-form itself, Terminator-style, into mayo.

MAKES 1½ CUPS

1 tablespoon freshly
    squeezed lemon
    juice
1 teaspoon kosher salt
½ teaspoon Dijon
    mustard
1 large egg yolk, at
    room temperature
1 ¼ cups vegetable oil

In a medium bowl, whisk together the lemon juice, salt, mustard, and egg yolk. Wrap a damp towel around the base of the bowl to keep it stable on the counter. Then, while whisking constantly, slowly and steadily drizzle in the vegetable oil until the mixture is thick. (You could also use a food processor for this.) This mayo will keep, covered and refrigerated, for up to 1 month.

Salad Dressings

You literally never have to buy salad dressing—making your own is cheaper and lets you flex all your control-freak tendencies. Some basic proportions: two parts oil to one part acid (lemon juice, vinegar, pickle juice all work) for a vinaigrette, and four parts yogurt to one part oil to one part acid for something yogurt-based. Pretty much any dressing base makes a killer marinade for meat or veggies before grilling or roasting. (Before you add any delicate or perishable add-ins to it—so, like, leave out the blue cheese or fresh tarragon or beluga caviar or whatever if you're using it to grill.)

Basic Vinaigrette

**MAKES ABOUT
½ CUP**

6 tablespoons olive oil
3 tablespoons red
    wine, white wine,
    or apple cider
    vinegar
Kosher salt and freshly
    ground black
    pepper

In a medium bowl, whisk together the oil and vinegar. Season with salt and pepper. This vinaigrette will keep, covered and at room temperature, for 3 to 5 days.

Blue Cheese Dressing

**MAKES ABOUT
1 CUP**

4 ounces blue cheese,
    crumbled
½ cup sour cream
⅓ cup mayonnaise
    (see page 24 or
    use store-bought)
¼ cup buttermilk
1 teaspoon onion
    powder
½ teaspoon granulated
    garlic
Kosher salt and freshly
    ground black
    pepper

In a medium bowl, combine the blue cheese, sour cream, mayo, buttermilk, onion powder, and granulated garlic. Season with salt and pepper. This dressing will keep, covered and refrigerated, for up to 5 days.

Miso Dressing

3 tablespoons white miso

2 tablespoons freshly squeezed lemon juice

In a medium bowl, whisk together the miso, lemon juice, and 3 tablespoons water until smooth. This dressing will keep, covered and refrigerated, for up to 1 week.

Homemade Ranch Dressing

¾ cup mayonnaise (see page 24 or use store-bought)

½ cup sour cream

2 tablespoons buttermilk

2 tablespoons finely chopped fresh parsley

2 tablespoons thinly sliced fresh chives

1 tablespoon finely chopped fresh dill

1 tablespoon white wine vinegar

1 teaspoon garlic powder

1 teaspoon onion powder

1 garlic clove, finely minced

1 shallot, peeled and finely chopped

Kosher salt and freshly ground black pepper

Combine all the ingredients except the salt and pepper in a medium bowl. Season with salt and pepper. This dressing will keep, covered and refrigerated, for up to 2 weeks.

Caesar Dressing

MAKES ABOUT
¾ CUP

1 garlic clove, peeled
and minced
Kosher salt
2 tablespoons freshly
squeezed lemon
juice
4 anchovy fillets,
minced
1 large egg yolk
½ cup olive oil
¼ cup freshly grated
Parmesan cheese
Freshly ground black
pepper

Put the garlic on a cutting board and sprinkle it with 1 teaspoon salt. Using the back of your knife, smash it into a paste. Transfer it to a medium bowl along with the lemon juice, anchovies, and egg yolk. Begin whisking and as you continue, slowly drizzle in the oil until the mixture is emulsified. Stir in the Parmesan cheese and a shitload of black pepper. Taste and season with more salt. This dressing will keep, covered and refrigerated, for 2 to 3 days.

Chicken Stock

To everyone out there paying $12 for a pint of bone broth, we've got news for you: [whispering] it's literally just chicken stock. And you can make it at home, freeze it, and use it whenever you need to braise something or make soup. Let the stock cool completely at room temperature before refrigerating or freezing. The chicken bones called for here can be cooked or uncooked: You can use the bones left over from the roast chicken (see page 56) or leftover bones if you break down your own chicken—and honestly, most butchers are happy to part with chicken necks and backs if you just ask nicely.

MAKES ABOUT
5 CUPS

1 pound chicken bones
10 sprigs parsley
10 whole black
    peppercorns
3 stalks celery, roughly
    chopped
2 large carrots, cut to fit
    into the pan
1 head garlic, halved
1 large onion, quartered
1 small bunch thyme

Put all of the ingredients in a large saucepan and cover with 10 cups water. Bring to a boil over high heat, then reduce the heat to a simmer. Cook, skimming off and discarding any scum that rises to the surface, for about 3 hours. Keep adding water as needed to keep the ingredients submerged. Strain through a fine-mesh sieve, discarding the solids. Cool completely before transferring to quart containers and refrigerating or freezing. Stock will keep frozen for up to 6 months and refrigerated for up to 1 week.

Sauces

In classic French cuisine, sauces are considered the building blocks for most dishes. In our universe, they play a slightly different role. While some, like béchamel, are the foundations of things like mac and cheese (page 51) and lasagna (pages 45–48), most of the others fall squarely into the "things that help other things taste good" category. Basically, all it takes is one of these to turn food from a collection of ingredients to a cohesive dish.

Béchamel Sauce

MAKES 3 CUPS

This is the basic white sauce that was the foundation of pretty much every casserole before they invented canned cream of mushroom soup, but don't hold that against it.

4 tablespoons
    unsalted butter
⅓ cup all-purpose flour
3 cups whole milk
Kosher salt and freshly
    ground black
    pepper

Melt the butter in a 6-quart saucepan over medium-high heat. Stir in the flour and cook for about 1 minute. Add the milk and cook, stirring occasionally, until the mixture thickens, 6 to 8 minutes. Season with salt and pepper. Béchamel will keep, refrigerated, for up to 5 days.

Peanut Sauce

MAKES ABOUT
1 CUP

This peanut sauce is good on everything—hell, we'd eat it off a shoe—but it's especially good over noodles with fried tofu and scallions. Or fold cooked rice noodles and leftover shrimp into it and finish with toasted sesame seeds, fresh cilantro, chopped peanuts, and a squeeze of lime. Your grocery store should have sambal amidst the chili sauces, and if it doesn't, grab some from an Asian market or online (or find a better grocery store).

½ cup smooth peanut
    butter
3 tablespoons sambal
2 tablespoons fish
    sauce

2 tablespoons soy
    sauce
1 tablespoon dark
    brown sugar

Whisk together all the ingredients in a medium bowl with ¼ cup water. Cover and refrigerate until ready to use. Peanut sauce will keep, refrigerated, for up to 2 weeks.

Cocktail Sauce

MAKES ABOUT
1 CUP

FYI, because it's confusing: fresh horseradish is found in the produce section; it looks like a large knobbly root, and if it were an emoji, the eggplant would be out of business. Prepared horseradish, which is what this recipe calls for and what gives cocktail sauce its trademark kick, is found in very civilized bottles, usually in the refrigerated section.

½ cup ketchup
3 tablespoons
    prepared
    horseradish
2 tablespoons freshly
    squeezed lemon
    juice

2 teaspoons
    Worcestershire
    sauce
Hot sauce

Combine all the ingredients in a bowl until well blended, adding hot sauce to taste. Cover and refrigerate until ready to use. The sauce will keep, refrigerated, for up to 7 days.

Barbecue Sauce

MAKES ABOUT
2 CUPS

So elsewhere in this book we tell you never to make ketchup. But you should absolutely put the food science ketchup geniuses' hard work to use to make this salty-sweet sauce that's killer on pulled pork (see page 205). You could also fold it into mayo for a dope spread for a steak sandwich.

2 cups ketchup
¼ cup granulated sugar
¼ cup packed light
    brown sugar
2 teaspoons freshly
    ground black
    pepper

2 teaspoons dry
    mustard powder
2 teaspoons onion
    powder
1 teaspoon kosher salt

Combine all the ingredients with 1 cup water in a medium saucepan over medium-high heat. Bring to a boil, then reduce the heat to maintain a simmer. Cook, stirring occasionally, until thick, about 45 minutes. This barbecue sauce will keep, refrigerated, for up to 1 month.

Arugula and Walnut Pesto

MAKES ABOUT
1 CUP

Sure, you can buy ready-made pesto, but it's so easy to make at home. It doesn't have to be basil (which is hard to come by in winter); that's why we call for arugula here. Parsley, mint, and cilantro all work great, too. If you want to be traditional, use pine nuts in place of walnuts and basil for the arugula. Extra pesto freezes well in ziplock bags or ice cube trays.

¾ cup roughly chopped
    walnuts
2½ ounces (3 cups)
    arugula
¼ cup grated Parmesan
    cheese

1 tablespoon freshly
    squeezed lemon
    juice
½ cup olive oil, plus
    more as needed
Kosher salt and freshly
    ground black
    pepper

Heat a large skillet over medium heat. Add the walnuts and cook until toasted and golden, 2 to 3 minutes. Cool and transfer to a food processor along with the arugula, cheese, and lemon juice. With the motor running, slowly drizzle in the ½ cup olive oil. Season with salt and pepper. Pesto can be stored in an airtight container with about a ¼-inch layer of additional olive oil to cover (to help keep the pesto green) for up to 5 days, refrigerated, or 3 months, frozen.

34 MUNCHIES Guide to Dinner

Tomato Sauce

This basic red sauce is the perfect answer to your Italian home-cooking dreams. It's the perfect accompaniment to calzones (see page 153) and is great smeared on the Grandma-Style Homemade Pizza (page 157). Or thin it out with some chicken stock (see page 31) or vegetable stock for a simple tomato soup. (Be sure to have a grilled cheese nearby for dipping.) And, of course, you can use it as-is for an easy weeknight pasta with just about anything added: Italian sausage, frozen spinach, sautéed mushrooms, or a splash of heavy cream all work nicely. Make a batch or two and freeze it so you have some on hand whenever the need arises. To defrost, simply move it to your fridge the night before, or run the container under cold water and slide the frozen block into a saucepan over low heat, stirring occasionally so that it doesn't burn.

2 tablespoons olive oil
2 garlic cloves, peeled and thinly sliced
1 small yellow onion, diced
Kosher salt
2 tablespoons tomato paste

2 tablespoons granulated sugar
1 (28-ounce) can whole peeled tomatoes, crushed by hand
½ cup loosely packed fresh basil leaves
2 tablespoons unsalted butter

Heat the oil in a medium saucepan over medium-high heat. Add the garlic and onion and season with salt. Cook until soft, 2 to 3 minutes. Add the tomato paste and cook 1 to 2 minutes more. Stir in the sugar and tomatoes and bring to a simmer. Reduce the heat to medium and cook, stirring occasionally, until thick, about 20 minutes. Season with salt and stir in the fresh basil and butter until melted. Cool slightly, then transfer to a blender or food processor and puree until smooth. Transfer to a container and cover. The tomato sauce will keep, refrigerated, for up to 1 week or frozen for up to 3 months.

Homemade Pasta

Making pasta from scratch might sound a little intimidating, but here's a super-straightforward, two-ingredient (and vegan!) method that we're really into. It's key to add the water slowly so the dough doesn't get too sticky, and you'll need a mixer with a dough hook to make this best. Be sure to let it rest for at least two hours before rolling it out. If you don't have a pasta roller, you can roll it out with a rolling pin (or wine bottle), but you'll end up with a more rustic, thick-cut pasta.

**MAKES ABOUT
1 POUND PASTA**

**2 cups semolina flour,
plus more for
dusting**

Mix the flour and ⅔ cup water in a mixer fitted with a dough hook, adding an additional tablespoon of water as needed, until smooth and lightly elastic. Wrap the dough in plastic wrap and refrigerate for at least 2 hours. Pasta dough will keep, refrigerated, for up to 5 days, or frozen for up to 3 months.

To form the pasta, divide the dough into four pieces. Lightly flour a work surface. Work with one piece at a time, keeping the remaining dough covered with a damp towel. Roll the piece through the second thinnest setting on a pasta machine and lay it on the work surface. Use your pasta roller's cutting attachment, a pizza cutter, or a sharp knife to cut each piece of dough into noodles, then dust the noodles well with semolina flour and gather them into a little nest. Put the nest on a floured surface and cover with a towel. Repeat with the remaining pieces of dough.

To cook fresh pasta, bring a large pot of seriously salted water to a boil. Cook for about 2 minutes, then drain.

Spinach, Mushroom, and Ricotta Ravioli

Ravioli are one of our favorite ways to put our homemade pasta dough to use. If you don't have time to make pasta dough (or didn't make any the night before), store-bought wonton wrappers work just fine. You can make the filled ravioli ahead of time: lay them out on parchment paper–lined baking sheets in your freezer, and once they're frozen, transfer them to freezer bags. Then whenever you're craving ravs, drop them, still frozen, into boiling water (they'll take a minute or two longer to cook than fresh). The filling here is an all-purpose mix that is also excellent in the Spinach and Mushroom Calzone (page 153) and the Spinach and Mushroom Lasagna (page 45).

MAKES ABOUT 4 DOZEN RAVIOLI

For the DOUGH
2 cups semolina flour, plus more for dusting

For the FILLING
2 tablespoons olive oil
1 small garlic clove, minced
½ small yellow onion, thinly sliced
Kosher salt
8 ounces cremini mushrooms, thinly sliced
5 ounces frozen spinach, defrosted, drained thoroughly, and roughly chopped
½ cup ricotta cheese
½ cup shredded mozzarella cheese
Freshly ground black pepper

For SERVING
Tomato Sauce (see page 35)
Freshly grated Parmesan cheese

Make the DOUGH: Mix the semolina and ⅔ cup water in a mixer fitted with a dough hook until smooth and lightly elastic. Wrap the dough in plastic wrap and refrigerate for at least 2 hours. Pasta dough will keep, refrigerated, for up to 5 days. Alternatively, freeze for up to 3 months.

Make the FILLING: Heat the oil in a large skillet over medium-high heat. Add the garlic and onion and season with salt. Cook until soft, about 2 minutes. Add the mushrooms and cook until soft, about 5 minutes more. Stir in the spinach and cook until mixed thoroughly, about 2 minutes more. Transfer to a sieve set over a bowl to drain, then transfer to a cutting board. Allow the vegetables to cool completely, then roughly chop them. Transfer the vegetables to a bowl with the ricotta and mozzarella, stir

continued

Spinach, Mushroom, and Ricotta Ravioli continued

together, and season with salt and pepper. Cover and refrigerate until ready to use.

Make the RAVIOLI: Divide the dough into four pieces. Lightly flour a work surface and a baking sheet with semolina flour. Work with one piece at a time, keeping the remaining dough covered with a damp towel. Roll the piece through the second thinnest setting on a pasta machine and lay it on the work surface. Place a row of 12 teaspoons of filling, 1 inch apart, along the bottom of each strip. Brush water around each spoonful of filling. Fold the top half of the strip over the bottom and press out any air pockets to seal in the filling. Cut out the ravioli. Transfer to the baking sheet dusted with semolina flour. Repeat with remaining balls of dough.

To SERVE: Heat the tomato sauce in a large skillet over medium-low heat. Bring a pot of generously salted water to a boil. Add the ravioli and cook until they float, 2 to 3 minutes. Transfer to the skillet of tomato sauce and toss to combine. Serve hot with Parmesan cheese.

Spinach and Mushroom Lasagna

Lasagna is the ultimate comfort food, the best way to feed a crowd (along with Garlic Bread, page 160), and the perfect gift for a friend who's going through some shit. (Deliver it frozen in a disposable tinfoil baking dish, and they can bake it when they need it: tell them to bake it straight from frozen for about 90 minutes at 350°F, then uncover and broil as in the recipe here.)

Feel free to swap out the spinach for a different green like chard or kale, or bulk it up with more mushrooms or another vegetable (butternut squash is a rich, tasty choice when it's cold out). Just cook the vegetables first before folding them into the mix.

SERVES 6 TO 8

For the FILLING
6 tablespoons olive oil
3 garlic cloves, minced
3 small yellow onions, thinly sliced
Kosher salt
3 pounds cremini mushrooms, thinly sliced
30 ounces frozen spinach, defrosted, drained thoroughly, and roughly chopped
6 cups shredded mozzarella
3 cups ricotta cheese
Freshly ground black pepper

For the BÉCHAMEL
4 tablespoons unsalted butter
⅓ cup all-purpose flour
4 cups whole milk
Kosher salt and freshly ground black pepper

For the LASAGNA
1 pound Homemade Pasta (page 37) or store-bought uncooked lasagna sheets
4 tablespoons olive oil
⅔ cup freshly grated Parmesan cheese

Make the FILLING: Heat the oil in a large saucepan over medium-high heat. Add the garlic and onions and season with salt. Cook until soft, about 4 minutes. Add the mushrooms and cook until soft, about 8 minutes more. Transfer the mushroom mixture to a colander to drain for 20 minutes, or until cool enough to handle. Then press out any remaining liquid. Transfer the mushrooms to a large bowl; add the spinach, 3 cups of the mozzarella, and the ricotta and season with salt and pepper.

Make the BÉCHAMEL: Melt the butter in a 6-quart saucepan over medium-high heat; add the flour and cook, stirring, for 2 minutes. Add the milk and cook, stirring occasionally, until thick, 8 to 10 minutes. Season with salt and pepper and combine with the mushroom mixture.

continued

Spinach and Mushroom Lasagna continued

Assemble the LASAGNA: If using store-bought pasta, bring a large pot of generously salted water to a boil. Add the lasagna sheets and cook until al dente, about 10 minutes. Drain, then toss gently with 2 tablespoons of the olive oil.

If using our homemade pasta, cut the dough into four pieces, keeping the other pieces covered with a cloth while you work with each piece. Press the piece into a rectangle that measures about 3 by 4 inches and feed it through the thickest roller setting on your pasta machine. Fold the dough into a rectangle and repeat, switching the setting down to one thinner after each go, until the dough has gone through the second-thinnest setting. Repeat with the remaining pieces of dough until you have four 5-inch-wide sheets of pasta measuring 2 to 3-feet long. Dust the sheets with semolina and trim each sheet into 13-inch lengths. Do not boil.

Heat the oven to 375°F. Drizzle the remaining 2 tablespoons of oil in the bottom of a 9 by 13-inch baking dish. If using store-bought pasta, lay 3 sheets of lasagna in the dish. If using homemade pasta, lay 2 sheets in the dish. Spread 2 cups of filling evenly over the pasta and sprinkle with ½ cup of the remaining mozzarella. Top with 3 more sheets of pasta (store-bought) or 2 more sheets of the pasta (homemade), and continue layering with filling and mozzarella. Once you get to the final layer (you should have 4 layers total), top with the remaining filling and the remaining 1 cup mozzarella, then the Parmesan. Cover loosely with aluminum foil and bake for 35 to 40 minutes. Remove the foil and turn the oven to broil. Cook the lasagna for another 5 minutes and remove from the oven. Let sit for 5 to 10 minutes before serving.

Beef Lasagna

Homemade Pasta (page 37) takes Garfield's go-to dish to the next level—just cut the rolled pasta sheets into 13-inch-long segments. But if you'd rather use store-bought pasta sheets, this will still be excellent. And on the nights when you don't want to deal with lasagna assembly, halve the meat sauce recipe and serve it on spaghetti.

SERVES 6 TO 8

For the
MEAT SAUCE

3 tablespoons olive oil, plus more for drizzling

3 garlic cloves, finely chopped

2 yellow onions, finely chopped

2 pounds ground beef

1 pound ground pork

¼ cup tomato paste

½ cup red wine

1 tablespoon granulated sugar

2 (28-ounce) cans pureed tomatoes

Kosher salt and freshly ground black pepper

For the BÉCHAMEL

1½ tablespoons unsalted butter

2 tablespoons all-purpose flour

2 cups whole milk

Kosher salt and freshly ground black pepper

3 cups ricotta cheese

1 cup shredded mozzarella cheese

For the LASAGNA

1 pound lasagna sheets or Homemade Pasta (see page 37)

4 tablespoons olive oil

1 cup shredded mozzarella cheese

1 cup freshly grated Parmesan cheese

Make the MEAT SAUCE: Heat olive oil in a large saucepan over medium-high heat. Add the garlic and onions and cook until soft, 3 to 4 minutes. Add the beef and pork and cook until browned, 6 to 8 minutes. Add the tomato paste and cook 2 minutes more. Add the red wine and cook until the wine has reduced, about 4 minutes. Add the sugar and tomatoes, reduce the heat to medium, and simmer until thick, about 20 minutes. Season with salt and pepper and set aside.

Make the BÉCHAMEL: Melt the butter in a medium saucepan over medium-high heat. Stir in the flour and cook for 1 to 2 minutes. Gradually add the milk, whisking constantly. Season to taste with salt and pepper and stir constantly with a wooden spoon until the sauce is the consistency of thick cream, about 15 minutes. Cool slightly, then combine with the ricotta, and mozzarella. Season with salt and pepper. Set aside.

continued

Beef Lasagna continued

Assemble the LASAGNA: If using store-bought pasta, bring a large pot of generously salted water to a boil. Add the lasagna sheets and cook until al dente, about 10 minutes. Drain, then toss gently with the 2 tablespoons of olive oil.

If using our homemade pasta recipe (page 37), cut the dough into 4 pieces, keeping the other dough pieces covered with a cloth while you work with each piece. Press the piece into a rectangle that measures about 3 by 4 inches and feed it through the thickest roller setting on your pasta machine. Fold the dough into a rectangle and repeat, switching the setting down to one thinner setting after each go until the dough has gone through the second-thinnest setting. Repeat with the remaining pieces of dough until you have four 5-inch-wide by 2- to 3-foot-long sheets of pasta. Dust the sheets with semolina flour and trim each sheet into 13-inch lengths. Do not boil.

Heat the oven to 375°F. Drizzle the remaining 2 tablespoons of olive oil in the bottom of a 9 by 13-inch baking dish. If using store-bought pasta, lay 3 sheets of lasagna in the dish. If using homemade pasta, lay two sheets in the dish. Spread 1 cup of béchamel evenly over the pasta and then 2 cups of the meat sauce. Top with 3 more sheets of the pasta (store-bought) or 2 more sheets of pasta (homemade), and continue layering with béchamel and meat sauce. Once you get to the final layer (you should have 4 layers total), top with the remaining 1 cup of meat sauce, the mozzarella, and the Parmesan. Cover loosely with aluminum foil and bake for 35 to 40 minutes. Remove the foil and turn the oven to broil. Cook the lasagna for another 5 minutes and remove from the oven. Let sit for 5 to 10 minutes before serving.

Macaroni and Cheese

Blue-box mac and cheese is delicious—we're not disputing that—but not-box mac and cheese is something you should also know how to make. Cellentani noodles are like fat, hollow spirals with the perfect ratio of sauce-retention to chew; if you can't find them, use your favorite shape. We're using Velveeta here, because it's the easiest, most un-fuck-up-able-est cheese to melt without turning into a grainy mess. The potato chips on top are kind of magical: they do everything you want breadcrumbs to do in this particular instance, like provide a crunchy counterpoint to the solid mass of béchamel and cheese you're putting in your face, but they do it better. (And hey, potato chips are gluten-free—which is clearly critical in a dish that's made of wheat noodles with a wheat flour–based sauce.) If this is all too much for you and you're sticking to the boxes you know and trust, our go-to ways of dressing up a boxed mac and cheese and helping ourselves feel like we're classy are (a) more cheese, stirred into the sauce before you fold the pasta in, (b) a swirl of pesto (see page 34) at the very end, (c) leafy greens like spinach or baby kale folded into the pasta to wilt so you can feel like you're being virtuous for eating vegetables, or (d) chopped, drained kimchi folded into the pasta.

SERVES 6 TO 8

4 tablespoons
  unsalted butter
⅓ cup all-purpose flour
4 cups whole milk
16 ounces Velveeta
  cheese, cubed
Kosher salt and freshly
  ground black
  pepper
1 pound cellentani
  pasta

3 cups plain potato
  chips, lightly
  crushed
½ cup grated Pecorino
  Romano cheese

Heat the oven to 375°F.

Melt the butter in a medium saucepan over medium-high heat. Add the flour and cook for about 1 minute. Add the milk and cook, stirring occasionally, until thick, 6 to 8 minutes. Stir in the Velveeta, salt, and pepper and cook until the cheese has melted.

continued

Macaroni and Cheese continued

Meanwhile, bring a large pot of salted water to a boil. Add the pasta and cook, stirring occasionally, until al dente, about 5 minutes. Drain the pasta, transfer to the cheese sauce, and stir well to coat.

Spread the pasta in a 9 by 13-inch baking pan and top with the chips and Pecorino cheese. Grind some fresh pepper over the top. Transfer the pan to a baking sheet and bake until the macaroni and cheese is golden brown and bubbly, about 15 to 20 minutes. Let cool for 10 minutes before serving.

How to Use Other Cheeses

If you're too good for Velveeta and want to use your fancy aged Comté or whatever, here's what you need to do: Order sodium citrate (basically a form of salt that helps cheese get melty) from the internet. Then, bring 1½ cups water to a simmer, and whisk in 2 teaspoons of the sodium citrate. Add a pound of your bougie grated cheese, whisking, again, to make sure it's all incorporated and melted. Fold in the cooked pasta, finish with the potato chips and Pecorino, and bake as usual. Or, you know, that's also why they invented Velveeta.

New York Strip Steak

Making a damn good steak is one of those basic life skills you probably could have used way more than, like, calculus. New York strip, sometimes called top sirloin or top loin, strikes a good balance between beefiness and tenderness—if you're super into tenderness, go for filet mignon; for ultra-beefy flavor, go for ribeye. And if you don't want to spend a ton of money, cuts like tri-tip, flatiron steak, and flank steak work with this precise method, too.

SERVES 2

2 New York strip steaks (about 1½ pounds total)
Kosher salt
2 tablespoons olive oil

Season the steaks all over generously with salt. We're not talking a sprinkling; we're talking a lot—about 3 tablespoons between the two strips. Leave them on a rack set over a sheet pan for at least 45 minutes. This helps draw the moisture out and sort of brines the steak, penetrating the meat, giving it more flavor and a better crust. If you don't have the luxury of time, salt the steak all over right before cooking.

Heat the oil in a large cast-iron skillet over medium-high heat. Make sure it gets hot! Add the steak and cook, flipping once, until you get a really nice color and crust, about 5 minutes for medium-rare. Using tongs, move the steak to a cutting board and allow it to rest for at least 10 minutes before slicing it against the grain.

Roast Chicken

Roast chicken is another one of those classic, perfect dishes that you've just gotta know how to make. It's best to dry and salt the chicken in the refrigerator overnight—this method gets you super-crispy skin—but even if you don't have the time to spare, it's not going to suck.

Tying the chicken's legs together with butcher's twine helps it cook more evenly, but even that's not mandatory, either. Basically, what we're trying to say is you don't have an excuse. Just roast a chicken. Once you're done eating, throw the bones into a freezer bag and freeze till you have time to make the stock on page 31.

If you have leftover chicken, it can go in a lot of things. Toss bite-size bits with mayo, chopped celery, scallions, and raisins (if you're a monster) and make chicken salad, or add them to a frittata (page 96), or use them in the Chicken Pot Pie (page 105) or the congee (page 85), or add them to the Pimento Cheese Quesadillas (page 118) or the calzone (page 153).

SERVES 4

**1 (3- to 4-pound)
chicken
Kosher salt**

Fit a baking sheet with a cooling rack. Pat the chicken dry with paper towels. Put it on the baking sheet breast side up and season liberally with the salt all over, including inside the cavity. Tuck the wings under the chicken and, using butcher's twine, tie the legs together. Don't cover the chicken. Refrigerate, ideally overnight (or leave at room temperature for an hour). The next day, let the chicken come to room temperature for 1 hour if you refrigerated it.

Heat the oven to 425°F. Roast the chicken for 1 hour, or until a thermometer inserted into the meatiest part of the thigh of the chicken reads 165°F. Transfer the chicken to a cutting board and let rest for 10 to 15 minutes before carving.

Baked Potato

The real joy in a baked potato is topping it with tons of stuff. Treat it like a steakhouse side with sour cream, bacon, and chives; hit it with the Chili Cheese Dip (page 120), or carb-load with a scoop of leftover Macaroni and Cheese (page 51). You can't go wrong. Dice leftover baked potatoes and crisp them up in a skillet with bacon fat and onion to make breakfast hash (finish with a fried egg), or brown some fresh chorizo, warm the potatoes alongside, and tuck it all into tacos, or make béchamel sauce (page 32), scoop out the potato flesh, and puree for a super easy, super-luxe-feeling potato soup (that you can—and should—finish with broccoli, cheddar, and probably bacon, too).

SERVES 4

4 large russet potatoes, scrubbed clean
2 tablespoons olive oil
Kosher salt

Heat the oven to 425°F. Put the potatoes on a small baking sheet and rub them all over with the oil and the salt. Pierce them a few times with the tines of a fork. Bake them until tender, 45 to 50 minutes.

(If you want less crispy skin wrap the potatoes in aluminum foil before baking.)

Don't have an oven? Pop them onto a microwave-safe dish and prepare them the same way (minus the foil). Cook them in the microwave on high for 5 minutes. Check to see if they're soft, and keep cooking, 2 minutes at a time, until tender.

Cheater's Rice

People mess up rice all the time. And we get it—most people are pretty dumb. But hey pal, you're not, and you take pride in your dinner. If you want to cook rice, the instructions on the box or bag work pretty well, tbh. If something goes irreparably wrong, there's always the congee on page 85.

MAKES 3 CUPS

1 cup white rice or brown rice

Bring a large pot of generously salted water (the rice will absorb the water, so you want to make the water taste good) to a boil. Add the rice and cook, stirring occasionally, until the rice is tender, exactly 12 minutes for white rice and 30 minutes for brown. Taste to check the texture and confirm that it's done; if not, give it a few more minutes. Drain well and serve immediately.

To REHEAT RICE: Put on a plate or in a microwave-safe bowl. Cover with a wet paper towel and microwave, stirring every minute or so, until warmed through. For a quick, easy dinner, add crunchy vegetables, toss with Miso Dressing (page 28), and finish with a fried egg.

To make RICE PUDDING: Simmer leftover rice in milk with a generous pinch of sugar and a cinnamon stick 'til it's tender, then stir in dried fruit and toasted nuts.

Mashed Potatoes

There are many ways to make mashed potatoes, and here's ours. The finer your mashing tool is, the less "rustic" your potatoes will be. If you have a ricer, that's how you get the ultra sleek, restaurant-style potatoes. A standard masher gets you a chunkier mash, while a wooden spoon gets you grandma-style. Food processors and blenders, meanwhile, get you glue, so do us a favor and don't mess this up with a food processor or blender. But if you have a stand mixer and really don't want to do work, that'll make some pretty soigné mashed potatoes, too. Mix leftovers up with an egg and panfry gently, flipping once, 'til both sides are golden brown, about 3 minutes per side—or use them to top the Chicken Pot Pie (page 105) in place of puff pastry.

SERVES 4 TO 6

3 pounds russet potatoes, peeled and cut into 1-inch pieces
Kosher salt
1¼ cups whole milk
6 tablespoons unsalted butter
Freshly ground black pepper

Cover the potatoes with water in a medium saucepan. Add 1 tablespoon salt and bring to a boil. Reduce the heat to maintain a simmer and cook until the potatoes are tender, about 20 minutes. Drain, then return the potatoes to the saucepan over medium heat and cook, stirring, to remove any excess moisture from the potatoes, 4 to 6 minutes. Stir in the milk and butter and mash using a potato masher. Season with salt and pepper and serve.

Buttermilk Fried Chicken Thighs

We know, we know—we have a fried chicken recipe in every one of our cookbooks (you should probably go buy those books and make those recipes, too). But this is an all-around great, keep-it-in-your-hat recipe for fried chicken. Using boneless chicken means it cooks more evenly, and using thighs (aka dark meat) means they'll taste dope. As an added bonus, the leftovers taste very nice on a sandwich the day after, or in the middle of the night.

6 cups buttermilk
12 boneless, skin-on
    chicken thighs
Vegetable oil, for
    deep-frying
2 cups all-purpose flour

Kosher salt and freshly
    ground black
    pepper
Hot sauce and honey,
    for serving

Put the buttermilk and chicken in a large container (make sure the chicken is fully submerged). Cover and refrigerate for 4 hours and up to 12 hours.

Heat 3 inches of vegetable oil in a large saucepan until a deep-fry thermometer reaches 350°F. Put the flour in a shallow dish and set up a cooling rack over a baking sheet. Remove the chicken from the buttermilk, shaking off excess. Put the chicken on the cooling rack. Season the chicken all over with salt and pepper, then dip each thigh into the flour and flip and turn until it's fully coated. Working in batches, fry the chicken, turning as needed, until a thermometer inserted into the thickest part of the chicken reads 165°F, 5 to 6 minutes. Transfer to a clean cooling rack set over a baking sheet and season with salt. Repeat with remaining chicken thighs and serve with hot sauce and honey.

Carne Asada Fries

Sure, you can eat fries by themselves. You can eat carne asada by itself, too. But this SoCal drunk food favorite exists for a reason, and that reason is that it's excellent. An initial water bath and a long, slow fry (starting out in cold oil) create perfectly crispy fries that hold up to even a major onslaught of toppings. And if you don't feel like frying, use tortilla chips instead of fries and turn these into nachos.

Heads up: The meat does need to marinate a while (all that citrus juice helps tenderize the meat so it's a good textural match for the fries), so you'll need to plan ahead for this. If you're really pressed for time, just the minimum hour of marinating will make all the difference.

For the CARNE ASADA

3 garlic cloves, roughly chopped
1 jalapeño, stemmed and roughly chopped
1 small bunch cilantro, leaves and tender stems roughly chopped
½ cup olive oil
2 tablespoons white vinegar
Kosher salt and freshly ground black pepper
3 limes, juiced
1 orange, juiced
1 pound flank steak

For the FRIES

2 pounds russet potatoes
Vegetable oil, for deep-frying
Kosher salt

For ASSEMBLING

1 cup Cotija cheese, crumbled
½ small white onion, finely diced
½ cup Pico de Gallo (see page 143)
½ cup Guacamole (see page 143)
½ cup fresh cilantro leaves
Lime wedges, for serving

Marinate the CARNE ASADA: Put the garlic, jalapeño, and cilantro in a food processor and pulse until finely chopped. Stir in the olive oil, vinegar, 2 teaspoons salt, 1 teaspoon pepper, and citrus juices and transfer to a large ziplock bag with the steak. Seal and refrigerate for at least an hour and up to 4 hours.

For the FRIES: Cut the potatoes into batons about ¼-inch thick around (you know, make it look like your favorite fast-food french fry). Put the potatoes in a large container filled with ice water for at least 1 hour. Line a sheet pan (or two if need be) with paper towels. Drain and rinse the potatoes, then spread out in a single layer onto the sheet pan and thoroughly blot dry with more paper towels.

continued

Carne Asada Fries continued

Put the potatoes in a large saucepan and cover with the vegetable oil. Turn the heat to medium and cook, stirring occasionally, until the potatoes are golden brown, about 40 minutes. Prep the sheet pan with fresh paper towels. Using a slotted spoon, transfer the fries to the sheet pan and season with salt. Keep warm in a 250°F oven.

Make a fire in a charcoal grill or preheat a gas grill to medium-high heat. Remove the steak from the marinade and season all over with salt and pepper. Grill, flipping once, until medium-rare, about 8 minutes. Transfer to a cutting board and let rest for 10 minutes before dicing.

For **ASSEMBLING**: Put the fries in a 9 by 13-inch baking dish or on a sheet pan. Top the fries with half of the cheese, then top with the diced meat and half of the diced onion. Top with the remaining cheese and the remaining onion, then the pico de gallo and guacamole. Sprinkle with the fresh cilantro leaves and serve with lime wedges.

On Frying

Don't act like you're above fried food. You know and we know that nearly everything that brings joy into the world is fried. A few things you should know about frying, though: Use a large, heavy pot, and never fill it more than halfway with oil. When you add the food, don't pack the pot so everything is touching each other; give everything a little breathing room to fry so they get properly crispy, and be sure to season everything savory with salt immediately after they come out of the fryer.

Good-for-Everything Chocolate Cake

Use this chocolate cake base as your go-to for birthday cakes, congratulations cakes, going-away cakes, welcome-home cakes, fuck-you cakes—whatever occasion calls for a cake. If making a cake is too daunting—it really shouldn't be, but if it is, okay, fine—you can totally use a boxed cake mix and achieve a similar, if maybe not as rich, result. To maximize your box mix, though, a couple of things: Use milk instead of water, melted butter instead of oil, and stir 2 tablespoons of mayo into the batter before baking. Sure, it sounds bizarre, but we promise the result will be more luxurious.

MAKES 1 (9-INCH) CAKE

1 cup all-purpose flour
1 cup granulated sugar
½ cup cocoa powder
1 teaspoon baking powder
1 teaspoon baking soda
½ teaspoon kosher salt
½ cup whole milk
¼ cup vegetable oil
1 teaspoon vanilla extract
1 large egg

Heat the oven to 375°F. Grease a 9-inch round cake pan and line with parchment paper. Grease the parchment paper. In a medium bowl, stir together the flour, sugar, cocoa powder, baking powder, baking soda, and salt. In a separate small bowl, whisk together the milk, oil, vanilla, and egg with 1 cup water. Using a hand mixer, beat the wet ingredients into the dry until smooth, then pour into the prepared pan. Bake for 35 minutes, or until a toothpick inserted in the middle comes out clean. Cool completely before frosting.

Chocolate Buttercream Frosting

Here's the classic buttercream you'll want to use for birthday cakes, cupcakes, or to eat with a spoon when it's been a rough night. It's a recipe, yeah, but fundamentally buttercream is a state of mind: keep an eye on the consistency and texture, adding milk as needed 'til it's the loosely fluffy frosting of your dreams. For white buttercream, swap the cocoa powder for more powdered sugar and hit with a drop or two more of vanilla extract. Gel food coloring—available at specialty baking shops or online—adds deep color without diluting the texture.

MAKES 3 CUPS, ENOUGH FOR ONE 2-LAYER CAKE

1 cup unsalted butter, cubed, at room temperature
1 pound confectioners' sugar, sifted
1 cup cocoa powder, sifted
½ teaspoon kosher salt
1 teaspoon vanilla extract
¼ cup whole milk

Put the butter in a large bowl with the sugar, cocoa powder, and salt. Using a hand mixer, beat the mixture until creamy, then add the vanilla and slowly add the milk until the frosting is light and fluffy. Use immediately or transfer to a container and cover. Refrigerate until ready to use, then soften at room temperature for at least 2 hours for an easy spreading consistency.

Meringue Cookies

This is one of those dead-easy, *holy shit I didn't realize this was all they were* recipes that it's never a bad idea to have in your back pocket. If you're not feeling cookies, add 2 teaspoons vinegar to the whipped whites, dollop on a sheet of parchment, and bake till dry, then top with whipped cream and fresh fruit to make a Pavlova, the queen of summer desserts.

MAKES 30

6 large egg whites
1 teaspoon cream of
tartar
1 cup granulated sugar

Heat the oven to 250°F. Line 2 baking sheets with parchment paper. Put the egg whites in a large bowl with the cream of tartar. Using a hand mixer or balloon whisk, whip the egg whites until foamy, about 2 minutes (much longer if using a whisk). Gradually beat in the sugar until the egg whites are glossy and stiff, 2 to 3 minutes more.

Dollop 2 tablespoons worth of meringue onto the parchment, spacing the meringues apart by about 1½ inches. Bake for 1 hour, until crisp on the outside. Meringues will keep in an airtight container for up to 1 week.

Separating Eggs

It's easiest with cold eggs, but whites whip best at room temperature, so plan ahead. Crack each egg and carefully let the white slide out into a ramekin or small bowl; then, tip the yolk back and forth between shell halves to coax out all the white. Then transfer that white to the larger bowl you'll use for whipping. The tiniest bit of yolk will prevent whites from whipping up properly, so the ramekin acts as insurance that you don't fuck up the whole batch.

WEEKNIGHT MEALS

Penne alla Vodka

This is a throwback '80s recipe that never should have gone out of style. For better or worse, the vodka's not going to get you drunk—it's ¼ cup, split among six servings—but it's also a myth that the alcohol totally burns off during cooking. Booze gives the sauce its characteristic sweetness, and no, you can't use bourbon or gin (or even tequila). This is called penne alla vodka for a reason, so you'll need to spare some for this recipe after you've made your jungle juice.

SERVES 4 TO 6

½ cup unsalted butter
1 medium yellow onion, diced
¼ cup vodka
1 (14.5-ounce) can crushed tomatoes
1 cup heavy cream

Kosher salt and freshly ground black pepper
1 pound penne pasta
Freshly grated Parmesan cheese, for serving
Fresh basil leaves, for serving

Melt the butter in a large skillet over medium heat. Add the onion and cook until soft, 3 to 4 minutes. Add the vodka and cook until evaporated, about 2 minutes. Add the tomatoes and cook, stirring occasionally, for 20 minutes. Add the cream and cook for 5 minutes more.

Meanwhile, bring a large pot of generously salted water to a boil. Add the pasta and cook until al dente, about 11 minutes. Drain well and transfer to the skillet with the sauce, tossing to coat. Season with salt and pepper and divide among individual bowls. Top with Parmesan cheese and basil to serve.

Bucatini with Sausage and Tomatoes

Pasta water is the secret ingredient in this recipe (and many other pasta recipes). When you boil pasta, it leaches starch into the water, which then turns into a magical substance that transforms a disparate pile of ingredients into a sleek, glossy sauce. Always save a cup of pasta water before you drain—if something's just not quite right with the final dish, a splash of pasta water is almost always the answer.

SERVES 6

1 pound bucatini
¼ cup olive oil
3 tablespoons unsalted butter
1 garlic clove, thinly sliced
1 small red onion, thinly sliced
1 pound spicy Italian sausage, casings removed
1 pound multicolored cherry tomatoes
½ teaspoon red pepper flakes

½ cup freshly grated Parmesan cheese, plus more for serving
Kosher salt and freshly ground black pepper
4 ounces fresh basil leaves

Bring a large pot of generously salted water to a boil. Add the pasta and cook until al dente, 9 minutes. Drain, saving ½ cup of the pasta water.

Meanwhile, heat 2 tablespoons of the oil and the butter in a large skillet over medium-high heat. Add the garlic and onion and cook until soft, about 7 minutes. Add the sausage and, using the back of a wooden spoon to break up the chunks of sausage, cook the sausage until browned, about 10 minutes. Using a slotted spoon, transfer the sausage, garlic, and onions to a bowl.

Add the remaining 2 tablespoons of olive oil and the tomatoes to the skillet and cook until the tomatoes are golden and begin to burst, about 7 minutes. Stir the sausage and onions back in, along with the pasta and the pasta water. Stir in the red pepper flakes and Parmesan cheese and season with salt and pepper. Quickly toss in the basil and divide among individual bowls. Serve with more Parmesan cheese.

Orecchiette with Pesto, Zucchini, and Eggplant

You may have heard that you absolutely must salt eggplant to make it less bitter, but it's actually an urban legend; we've cooked a lot of eggplant and have rarely encountered any bitter enough to need salting. The real trick here is being patient enough to let it fully cook through, so it transforms from fibrous to silky smooth.

SERVES 6

1 pound orecchiette

¼ cup olive oil

2 medium zucchini, cut into 1-inch pieces

Kosher salt and freshly ground black pepper

1 medium eggplant, cut into 1-inch pieces

1 ½ cups heavy cream

1 cup Arugula and Walnut Pesto (page 34)

2½ ounces arugula

Zest and juice of 1 lemon

¾ cup roughly chopped walnuts, toasted

Parmesan cheese, to serve

Bring a large pot of generously salted water to a boil. Add the pasta and cook until al dente, about 8 minutes. Drain the pasta, reserving ½ cup of pasta water.

Meanwhile, heat 2 tablespoons of the oil in a large skillet over high heat. Add the zucchini and sauté until golden, about 10 minutes. Season with salt and pepper and transfer to a bowl.

Heat the remaining olive oil in the skillet and add the eggplant. Cook, tossing occasionally, until golden, about 10 minutes. Season with salt and pepper, then return the zucchini to the skillet along with the cream. Bring to a boil, then reduce the heat to maintain a simmer. Cook until the cream has thickened, about 2 minutes. Add the pesto and the pasta and toss to combine. Add the arugula, lemon zest, and lemon juice and season with salt and pepper. If needed, add some reserved cooking liquid to achieve a creamy consistency. Serve immediately, topped with the walnuts and Parmesan cheese.

Shrimp and Chickpea Salad

This is one of those super-fast, easy-as-hell dinners that you can serve to unexpected company without feeling even the slightest amount of shame. If you want to be an overachiever and cook the chickpeas yourself, soak ½ cup dried chickpeas overnight in a big bowl of water (bigger than you think you'll need) with a pinch of baking soda, then drain them, add them to a pot with fresh water to cover generously, and simmer them for 2 hours or until tender.

Vegans lost their collective shit a few years ago when they realized that the liquid from canned chickpeas (called aquafaba) actually behaves a lot like egg whites when whipped, meaning—voilà!—a whole new world of vegan-friendly dessert options. If you're feeling ambitious, save the liquid to make a vegan version of Meringue Cookies (see page 72).

SERVES 4

½ small red onion, thinly sliced
20 medium shrimp, peeled and deveined
Kosher salt and freshly ground black pepper
¼ cup olive oil
2 ripe avocados, halved, pitted, peeled, and cut into 1-inch chunks
1 English cucumber, halved lengthwise, seeded, and thinly sliced
2 limes
1 (15.5-ounce) can chickpeas, rinsed and drained
½ bunch cilantro, torn into bite-sized sprigs

Put the red onion in a small bowl and cover with cold water. Let sit for 10 minutes to take out some of the bite of the onion. Drain, discarding the water, and put the onion in a large serving bowl.

Season the shrimp all over with salt and pepper. Heat 2 tablespoons of the oil in a large skillet over medium-high heat. Add the shrimp and cook, flipping once, until pink and lightly golden on each side, about 7 minutes. Add them to the bowl with the onions and allow the shrimp to cool slightly.

Add the avocado chunks and cucumber slices to the shrimp and onion. Squeeze some lime juice over the avocado. Add the remaining 2 tablespoons of olive oil, the chickpeas, and the cilantro and toss gently to combine. Season with salt and pepper and more lime juice.

Congee with Chicken and Scallions

So on page 61 we talk about how it's very easy to fuck up rice. But one truly magical thing about rice is that if you do overcook it, all you have to do is keep cooking it, and eventually you'll end up with congee. This good-with-everything rice porridge is typically eaten for breakfast under many different names throughout East Asia. Adding both Crispy Garlic and Crispy Shallots (pages 18 and 21) gives the final dish both depth and texture, but we're not the boss of you; add whatever you want. This congee works beautifully with sautéed mushrooms or other vegetables, a poached egg, and a sprinkle of togarashi or toasted sesame seeds.

SERVES 4

6 bone-in, skinless chicken thighs
10 cups chicken stock (see page 31)
1 bunch scallions, root ends trimmed
1½ cups long grain white rice
2 tablespoons fish sauce
Crispy Garlic (page 18)
Crispy Shallots (page 21)
Chili oil

Put the chicken thighs in a large saucepan and cover with the chicken stock. Halve three of the scallions crosswise and add to the saucepan. Bring to a low simmer and cook, slightly covered, until the chicken is tender and falling off the bone, about 1 hour. Strain, discarding the scallions, and set the chicken aside to cool slightly. Pick the meat from the bones, discarding the bones. You should have about 9 cups of stock.

Put the stock back in the saucepan along with the rice. Bring to a boil, then reduce the heat to maintain a simmer. Cook until the rice is overcooked and the soup is thick, adding water as needed, 35 minutes. Stir the chicken back through the congee and season with the fish sauce.

Thinly slice the remaining scallions, both white and green parts, and divide the congee among individual plates. Garnish the congee with the sliced scallions and the crispy garlic and shallots. Drizzle with chili oil before serving.

Pork Schnitzel with Fennel and Olive Salad

The major skill we're hoping you will confidently take away from this recipe is breading, which you can then apply to breading chicken cutlets, steak, or slabs of eggplant or zucchini. Use one hand for dry ingredients and one hand for wet, or you'll turn into a clumpy humanoid mess of flour and breadcrumbs . . . Don't say we didn't warn you.

SERVES 6 TO 8

For the SALAD
3 tablespoons olive oil
1 tablespoon Dijon mustard
1 tablespoon whole-grain mustard
1 tablespoon white wine vinegar
Kosher salt and freshly ground black pepper
1 bulb fennel, thinly sliced, fronds reserved
1 bunch frisée (about 6 ounces)
½ cup pitted kalamata olives, crushed by hand

For the PORK
3-pound boneless pork butt, trimmed
1½ cups all-purpose flour
Kosher salt and freshly ground black pepper
4 large eggs, lightly beaten
3 cups dried plain breadcrumbs
2 cups vegetable oil

Prepare the SALAD: In a large bowl, whisk together the oil with the mustards and vinegar. Season with salt and pepper and set aside.

Put the fennel slices in a medium bowl and cover with ice water for 15 minutes, then drain and pat dry. Set aside until ready to serve.

Make the PORK: Cut the pork into ½-inch thick slices. Roll out plastic wrap onto a work surface. Put one slice of pork on the plastic wrap and cover with another piece of plastic wrap. (Or place it in a gallon-size ziplock bag, leaving the bag unsealed.) Using a meat tenderizer, hammer, or rolling pin, pound the pork until thin, about ¼-inch thick.

continued

Pork Schnitzel with Fennel and Olive Salad continued

Meanwhile, put the flour in a large bowl and season generously with salt and pepper. Put the eggs and breadcrumbs into two separate bowls. Working with one piece of pork at a time, put it first in the flour, then the egg (make sure it coats it completely!), then the breadcrumbs. And for those of you who didn't read our warning above, remember: use one hand for dry ingredients and one hand for wet, or you'll probably regret it. Transfer to a plate and repeat with all the pieces of pork.

Heat the oil in a large skillet over medium heat and line a plate with paper towels. Working in batches, fry the pork, flipping once, until golden brown, about 5 to 7 minutes. Remove from the pan and transfer to the paper towel–lined plate. Season with salt and repeat with the remaining pieces of pork.

To serve, toss the fennel and frisée in the dressing along with the olives. Transfer the pork to a platter and top with the salad. Garnish with the fennel fronds.

Coconut Fish Curry

All curries are a process of building flavors on top of each other, including this one (even though it's quick AF). The secret here is to add the ingredients in the order in which they're listed, and let each one cook before adding the next. But once the fish goes in, it's time to be gentle; if you mix it up too much, it'll all fall apart. Just lay the fillets on top of the vegetables, cover, and let it go.

SERVES 4

3 garlic cloves, peeled and smashed

1 (2-inch) piece fresh ginger, peeled and finely chopped

Kosher salt

1½ pounds skinless white fish fillets, like cod, hake, or haddock, cut into 2-inch pieces

3 tablespoons vegetable oil

1 medium yellow onion, thinly sliced

1 tablespoon curry powder

3 tomatoes, cored and cut into 1½-inch pieces

3 tablespoons white vinegar

2 small red or green chiles, stemmed and thinly sliced

1 medium Japanese eggplant, cut into 1-inch pieces

1 (13.5-ounce) can coconut milk

Steamed jasmine rice, to serve

Fresh cilantro leaves, for garnish

Put the garlic and ginger on a cutting board and sprinkle with 1 tablespoon salt. Using the back of the knife blade, smash the garlic and ginger into a paste. Set aside.

Season the fish with salt and set aside. Heat the oil in a large saucepan over medium-high heat. Add the onion and cook until soft, about 3 minutes. Add the garlic and ginger paste and the curry powder and cook until fragrant, 1 to 2 minutes more. Stir in the tomatoes and cook until just soft, about 2 minutes. Stir in the vinegar, chiles, eggplant, and coconut milk and bring to a simmer. Cook until the eggplant is soft, about 12 minutes. Place the fish on top of the curry. Cover, then reduce the heat to medium-low and cook until the fish is cooked through, 8 to 10 minutes. Serve with steamed rice and garnish with cilantro leaves.

Lemongrass-Steamed Mussels

It's incredibly hard to overstate the late Anthony Bourdain's profound influence on the contemporary food world, but it's even harder to overstate how shitless he scared the food-loving public about eating shellfish in restaurants with his 2000 memoir, *Kitchen Confidential*. (Not on a Monday, not in a box, not with a fox. Not ever.) But if you're buying good shellfish and cooking them yourself, you've got one of the quickest, easiest, most decadent-feeling meals you can stuff in your face, minus the fear of the unknown.

Buy your mussels the day you want to eat them, then give them a good scrub in cold water and pull off their "beards" (the little fuzzy bits growing out of the crack in the shell) if they have them. And there are still a couple of rules: Don't cook any mussels that are open and don't close after you tap them firmly, and don't eat any mussels that don't open once they are cooked.

SERVES 4

For the MUSSELS
3 tablespoons olive oil
5 garlic cloves, peeled and thinly sliced
3 medium shallots, peeled and thinly sliced
1 small red chile, stemmed and thinly sliced
1 stalk lemongrass, thinly sliced
1 (2-inch) piece fresh ginger, peeled and finely chopped
Kosher salt

2 pounds mussels, cleaned
1 (12-ounce) bottle lager or light beer
Fresh cilantro leaves, for garnish

For the GRILLED BREAD
8 slices crusty bread, cut 1½ inches thick
3 tablespoons olive oil
1 garlic clove, halved crosswise
Kosher salt

Make the MUSSELS: Heat the olive oil in a large saucepan over medium-high heat. Add the garlic, shallots, chile, lemongrass, and ginger and season with salt. Cook until soft, about 5 minutes. Add the mussels and the beer, cover, and cook until the mussels have opened, about 5 minutes. Garnish with the cilantro leaves.

Make the GRILLED BREAD: Meanwhile, drizzle the bread all over with the olive oil. Heat a grill pan on high and grill the bread, flipping once, until charred, 3 to 4 minutes. Rub the bread with the cut side of the garlic and season with salt. Serve with the mussels.

Cast-Iron Skillet Salmon with Miso Dressing

SERVES 2

"One-pan dinners" has kind of a grim, Stepford vibe, like you're going to end up with some sort of greyish casserole or something, but this is a one-pan dinner you can be legitimately proud to serve. Letting the salmon hang out in the refrigerator on a sheet pan for an hour helps the skin dry enough to crisp up properly; if you don't have the time, you can skip this step, but crispy salmon skin is an enjoyable thing to have. The extra dressing you'll have left over from the basic recipe is also wonderful on roasted asparagus or burst cherry tomatoes, or to dress up a lunch salad.

2 (8-ounce) skin-on
    salmon fillets
3 tablespoons
    vegetable oil
Kosher salt
4 ounces shiitake
    mushrooms, stems
    removed
2 heads baby bok
    choy, quartered
    lengthwise and
    sliced into 1-inch
    pieces
½ cup Miso Dressing
    (page 28)

¼ teaspoon toasted
    black sesame seeds
¼ teaspoon toasted
    white sesame seeds
1 scallion, white
    and green parts,
    trimmed and thinly
    sliced

Put the salmon fillets skin-side up on a paper towel–lined plate and refrigerate for 1 hour.

Heat the oven to 350°F. Heat 2 tablespoons of the oil in a large cast-iron skillet over medium-high heat. Score the salmon skin and season the salmon all over with salt. Add the salmon to the skillet, skin-side down, and cook, gently pressing down on the flesh side using a fish spatula, until the skin is crispy, 5 to 7 minutes. Transfer the salmon, skin-side up, to a plate. Add the shiitake mushrooms to the skillet with the remaining 1 tablespoon oil and cook until lightly golden, about 3 minutes. Toss in the bok choy and cook for 2 to 3 minutes longer. Stir in ¼ cup of the miso dressing and toss to combine. Put the salmon on top, skin side up, and put the skillet in the oven. Roast until the salmon is cooked through, 5 to 7 minutes. Remove from the oven and sprinkle with the sesame seeds and scallion. Serve with the remaining ¼ cup miso dressing.

Mint and Pea Frittata with Sumac

A frittata is basically a quiche minus the crust, and losing the crust turns the dish from a fussy brunch item to an any-night dinner. The frozen peas in here should be a staple in your freezer, not just for icing your spinning or skateboarding injuries, but for adding to recipes that could use a little more green stuff.

Sumac is a spice—technically a fruit if you're going on *Jeopardy* any time soon, but for all intents and purposes, a spice—from the Middle East that adds complex brightness to anything and everything. If there's no sign of it at the grocery store, you should be able to find it at a specialty spice shop online. Just don't skip it; we promise it's worth finding.

SERVES 4

12 eggs, lightly beaten
4 ounces feta cheese, crumbled
1 cup frozen peas, defrosted
½ cup Greek yogurt
⅓ cup roughly chopped fresh dill
2 tablespoons finely chopped fresh mint
1½ teaspoons kosher salt
Freshly ground black pepper
Sumac, for serving

Heat the oven to 425°F. In a large bowl, whisk the eggs with the feta, peas, yogurt, dill, mint, salt, and pepper. Transfer to a 10-inch nonstick oven-safe skillet and bake until the eggs have puffed and are golden brown, 35 minutes. Cool slightly.

To remove from the skillet, slide a rubber spatula between the frittata and the skillet. Put a cutting board on top of the skillet and carefully flip it over. Sprinkle with the sumac and cut into wedges to serve.

Alternatively, serve it directly out of the skillet (just be sure it has cooled enough to touch).

Eggs in Purgatory

You've probably seen some version of this at the kind of airy, mimosa-serving brunch places your #influencer acquaintances eat at. This bright, tangy tomato sauce freezes very well; double the batch and freeze a little extra (minus the eggs) for an ultra-easy supper on the nights you can't be bothered to do more.

SERVES 2 TO 4

5 tablespoons olive oil, plus more for drizzling

4 garlic cloves, thinly sliced

1 medium yellow onion, thinly sliced

Kosher salt and freshly ground black pepper

1 teaspoon red pepper flakes

1½ pounds multicolored cherry tomatoes

6 large eggs

6 thick slices country bread

1 small bunch basil, leaves picked, for garnish

Heat 2 tablespoons of the olive oil in a large skillet over medium-high. Add the garlic and onion and season with salt and pepper. Cook until the onion is soft, about 3 minutes. Add the red pepper flakes and cook for 1 to 2 minutes, then stir in the tomatoes. Reduce the heat to medium and cook, stirring, until the tomatoes begin to burst (use a wooden spoon to smash them a bit) and they start to thicken, about 10 minutes. Season with salt and pepper.

Make six little wells in the tomatoes and crack one egg into each well. Season the eggs with salt and pepper, cover the pan, and reduce the heat to low. Cook until the whites of the eggs are set but the yolks are still runny, about 7 minutes.

Meanwhile, heat a grill pan or large cast-iron skillet over high heat. Drizzle the bread with the remaining 3 tablespoons olive oil and grill, flipping once, until charred, about 4 minutes. Season with salt and set aside.

To serve, drizzle a bit more oil over the top of the eggs and sprinkle with the basil leaves. Serve alongside the toasted bread.

Burnt Broccoli with Tahini-Mustard Dressing

The broiler is an underrated tool when it comes to getting dinner on the table quickly—you can have this ready to eat faster than the average oven comes to temperature. Don't be afraid to really char the hell out of the broccoli—that's what gives the dish character. Drop this on a bowl of rice with a poached egg and feel like you're performing self-care.

SERVES 4

¼ cup tahini
3 tablespoons white wine vinegar
2 tablespoons whole-grain mustard
1 tablespoon Dijon mustard
Kosher salt and freshly ground black pepper

2 pounds broccoli, cut into florets, stems cut into ¼-inch disks
2 tablespoons olive oil

In a large bowl, whisk together the tahini, vinegar, and mustards along with 2 tablespoons water. Season with salt and pepper and set aside.

Heat the oven to broil. Toss the broccoli with the olive oil, salt, and pepper on a baking sheet. Broil, tossing the broccoli once halfway through, until blackened, about 10 minutes. Toss the broccoli with the dressing to coat. Transfer to a platter and serve immediately.

Charred Cabbage with Hazelnuts

Cabbage (and other types of brassica, like the Burnt Broccoli with Tahini-Mustard Dressing, page 102) completely transforms when you burn the fuck out of it. (If you don't believe us, just ask any '00s "gastropub" chef selling deep-fried brussels sprouts.) It goes from being green and vegetal to deeply savory, its flavor transitioning from side to main dish–worthy. The anchovies add an earthy depth here; if you're serving this to vegetarians or vegans, you can approximate this by swapping out the anchovies for a teaspoon of miso paste.

SERVES 4

10 tablespoons olive oil
3 tablespoons freshly squeezed lemon juice
2 tablespoons capers, rinsed, drained, and finely chopped
1 teaspoon ground turmeric
4 anchovies, mashed into a paste
Freshly ground black pepper
½ head green cabbage, cut into 8 wedges

Kosher salt
2 tablespoons roughly chopped toasted hazelnuts, for garnish
1 or 2 sprigs basil, leaves picked, for garnish
1 sprig parsley, leaves picked, for garnish

In a medium bowl, whisk together 6 tablespoons of the olive oil with the lemon juice, capers, turmeric, and anchovies. Season with a shitload of black pepper. Set the dressing aside.

Heat the oven to broil. Drizzle the cabbage all over with the remaining 4 tablespoons of oil and season with salt and pepper. Broil the cabbage, flipping once halfway, until blackened, about 13 minutes. Transfer to a platter and drizzle with the dressing. Garnish with the nuts and herbs and serve immediately.

Crispy Green Beans with Toban Djan

Toban djan (also called doubanjiang) is a Sichuan chili bean paste that's an incredible building block for rich, spicy flavor. Keep a jar in the fridge and add some to pork or beef marinades, stir-fry a blob of it with leftover rice and top with a fried egg, or toss cubed potatoes in it before roasting in a hot oven until crispy. Here, it adds heat and funk to green beans. You can find it in most grocery stores, but worst-case scenario, seek out an Asian market, where you can also pick up jars of crispy shallots and garlic if you don't want to fry them yourself.

SERVES 4

1 pound green beans,
    trimmed
Olive oil
Kosher salt and freshly
    ground black
    pepper
2 tablespoons toban
    djan
1 tablespoon toasted
    white sesame
    seeds

Crispy Garlic (page 18)
Crispy Shallots
    (page 21)

Heat the oven to broil. On a baking sheet, toss together the green beans, oil, salt, and pepper. Broil, stirring once halfway through, until charred and blackened slightly in places, 5 to 7 minutes. Cool slightly, then toss with the toban djan and sesame seeds. Transfer to a platter and top with the crispy garlic and shallots.

Chicken Pot Pie

Okay, we get that this doesn't sound like a weeknight meal, but we swear it is. If you have the chicken stock already made (see page 31, or just buy some), you can throw this together using a store-bought rotisserie chicken or leftover shredded chicken from another meal. Or, if you insist on being an overachiever, make this on a weekend and split the pie into smaller portions in individual containers (like larger ramekins or little foil trays), and freeze them. Just move what you'll want the next day into the refrigerator to thaw overnight, then bake it when you need it. It's rich, so an acidic salad goes super nicely alongside.

SERVES 6 TO 8

For the CHICKEN STOCK
- 1 (3- to 4-pound) whole chicken
- 2 medium carrots, roughly chopped
- 2 stalks celery, chopped
- 1 head garlic, halved
- 1 yellow onion, quartered

For the POT PIE
- 8 tablespoons unsalted butter
- 2 medium carrots, diced
- 1 medium yellow onion, diced
- 12 ounces button mushrooms, quartered
- ¾ cup all-purpose flour
- 2 cups whole milk
- 3 cups shredded chicken (use the chicken meat if you've just made stock)
- 1 cup fresh or frozen peas, defrosted
- Kosher salt and freshly ground black pepper
- 14 ounces frozen puff pastry, thawed but refrigerated and chilled
- 1 large egg, lightly beaten

Make the CHICKEN STOCK: Put the chicken in a large pot and cover with water. Add the carrots, celery, garlic, and onion and bring to a boil. Reduce to a simmer and cook until the chicken is tender, about 1½ hours. Using tongs, transfer the chicken to a baking sheet to cool. Once the chicken is cool enough to handle, pick all of the meat off of the bones, discarding the bones and skin. Strain the stock, discarding the remaining solids. Set aside 2 cups of stock, saving or freezing the rest for another use.

continued

Chicken Pot Pie continued

Make the POT PIE: Heat the oven to 375°F. Melt the butter in a medium saucepan over medium heat. Add the carrots and onion and cook until the carrots are soft, about 5 minutes, then add the mushrooms. Cook for another 3 minutes, then add the flour. Cook for 2 to 3 minutes, then slowly add the reserved stock and the milk. Cook, stirring, until thick, 6 to 7 minutes. Stir in the reserved shredded chicken and the peas and season with salt and pepper. Transfer to a 9 by 13-inch casserole dish and spread in an even layer. Top with the puff pastry and cut a few 1-inch slits in the top. Brush with the beaten egg and bake until the pastry crust is puffed and golden, about 45 minutes. Cool slightly before serving.

Beef Satay with Peanut Sauce

Fresh lemongrass gives this dish its characteristic tanginess. Look for it in the vegetable section: it looks like a long, dry, skinny leek. Peel back the tough outer layers and dice the tender inner bits.

For the STEAK AND MARINADE
1 tablespoon finely chopped lemongrass
1 tablespoon fish sauce
1 tablespoon soy sauce
2 teaspoons light brown sugar
1½ teaspoons ground turmeric
½ teaspoon ground cumin
1 garlic clove, minced
1 (1-inch) piece fresh ginger, peeled and minced
1½ pounds flank steak, cut into ½-inch strips
Kosher salt

For SERVING
½ cup toasted and salted peanuts, chopped
Cilantro leaves, for garnish
Peanut Sauce (page 33)

Marinate the STEAK: In a medium bowl, whisk together the lemongrass, fish sauce, soy sauce, brown sugar, turmeric, cumin, garlic, and ginger. Add the steak, tossing to coat completely. Cover and refrigerate for at least 1 hour.

Make the BEEF SATAY: Thread the beef onto skewers and season all over with salt. Make a fire in a charcoal grill or preheat a gas grill to medium-high heat. Cook the satay, flipping once, until charred on each side, 5 minutes. Transfer to a platter and sprinkle with the peanuts and cilantro leaves. Serve with peanut sauce for dipping.

WEEKEND ENTERTAINING

Binge-Watching Party

BINGE-WATCHING PARTY

Binging the most recent season of your favorite show before the new season's episodes hit the air requires dedication, endurance, and, of course, snacks. Good ones! For a proper twelve-hour session of *Game of Thrones* where you attempt to remember all of the characters' subplots and who's banging whom, you're gonna need more than that half-empty bag of stale pretzels hanging out in your pantry. (We didn't include a beverage for this party menu, because nothing's worse than a constant barrage of bathroom break requests just when things are really starting to pop off on screen. But, you know, be a good host and don't let your guests get dehydrated.)

Onion Dip

Restaurant chefs and recipe testers with high-powered stoves and burners the circumference of a watermelon will tell you that it takes only 5 or 10 minutes to properly caramelize onions, but that is one big fat lie for the average home cook. For our purposes here, budget at least 15 to 20 minutes (since we are only lightly caramelizing them). Don't slice them too thinly, don't overcrowd your pan, and for heaven's sake, don't crank the heat up all the way! Just let them hang out and be patient. You'll thank us later.

**MAKES ABOUT
2 CUPS**

2 tablespoons olive oil
1 bunch scallions, white and green parts, trimmed and thinly sliced
1 small yellow onion, thinly sliced
1½ cups sour cream
½ cup mayonnaise (see page 24) or use store-bought
2 tablespoons thinly sliced chives
1 tablespoon freshly squeezed lemon juice
1 tablespoon onion flakes
1 tablespoon Worcestershire sauce
1 teaspoon onion powder
Kosher salt and freshly ground black pepper
Potato chips, for serving

Heat the olive oil in a small skillet over medium-high heat. Add the scallions and onion and cook until golden, about 3 minutes. Reduce the heat to medium and cook until lightly caramelized, 15 to 20 minutes. Let cool completely.

In a large bowl, combine the sour cream, mayonnaise, chives, lemon juice, onion flakes, Worcestershire sauce, onion powder, salt, and pepper with the caramelized onions. Transfer to a bowl and refrigerate for at least 1 hour before serving with the chips.

Pimento Cheese Quesadillas

Pimentos, or cherry peppers, are cute little round red peppers that rank just below poblanos in spiciness. In other words, they're not hot, really, so don't be intimidated. If you're not hungry enough to make and eat nine quesadillas, save some of the cheese (the recipe makes 3 cups) for another binge-worthy night and use it as a spread for crackers like they do down South. Pro tip: the cheese spread goes onto the tortillas easier when it's at room temperature.

MAKES 9 QUESADILLAS

8 ounces aged cheddar cheese, grated

8 ounces sharp cheddar cheese, grated

¼ cup mayonnaise (see page 24) or use store-bought

½ teaspoon cayenne pepper

1 (4-ounce) jar pimentos, rinsed and drained, then finely chopped

Kosher salt and freshly ground black pepper

18 (8-inch) flour tortillas

6 tablespoons olive oil

In a medium bowl, mix the cheeses with the mayonnaise, cayenne, and pimentos. Season with salt and pepper. The pimento cheese will keep, covered and refrigerated, for up to 1 week.

Working with one tortilla at a time, spread ⅓ cup of the pimento cheese mixture on one side. Top with another tortilla. Heat 2 teaspoons olive oil in a 10-inch nonstick skillet over medium heat. Cook, flipping once, until the tortillas are golden and crispy, 3 to 4 minutes. Transfer to a cutting board and cut into six wedges. Repeat with the remaining tortillas and cheese. Serve hot.

Chili Cheese Dip

If you skip the cream cheese step here, you can also serve this recipe as just regular old chili, with some sour cream, cheddar cheese, and sliced scallions for garnish. Bonus: Chili freezes extremely well, so you can keep extra portions of this recipe frozen in sealed containers for months at a time. We recommend that you make a huge batch to sustain you through many winter nights.

2 tablespoons olive oil
1 small yellow onion, finely chopped
2 garlic cloves, thinly sliced
2 tablespoons tomato paste
1 pound ground beef
½ cup light beer
2 tomatoes, cored and finely chopped
1 (13.5-ounce) can black beans, rinsed and drained
4 ounces cream cheese
1 cup shredded cheddar cheese
Kosher salt and freshly ground black pepper
2 scallions, white and green parts, trimmed and thinly sliced
Tortilla chips, for serving

Heat the oil in a large skillet over medium-high heat. Add the onion and cook until soft, about 3 minutes. Add the garlic and cook for 1 minute more, then stir in the tomato paste and cook for 1 to 2 minutes. Add the beef and cook, breaking the meat up with a wooden spoon, until browned, about 4 minutes. Add the beer, tomatoes, and beans and cook until the tomatoes have broken down and the chili is thick, about 6 minutes. Stir in the cream cheese and cook until melted, about 2 minutes, then remove from the heat and stir in the cheddar. Season with salt and pepper and sprinkle with the scallions. Serve hot with the tortilla chips.

Cacio e Pepe Popcorn

If you're really, truly skeptical of your ability to make popcorn on the stove, we will understand if you just go ahead and buy microwaveable unbuttered popcorn and garnish it with this eternally delicious combination of butter, cheeses, salt, and pepper. But we promise it's not hard.

SERVES 6

3 tablespoons
   vegetable oil
¾ cup popcorn kernels
6 tablespoons unsalted
   butter, melted
¼ cup grated Pecorino
   Romano cheese
3 tablespoons freshly
   grated Parmesan
   cheese

2 teaspoons freshly
   ground black pepper
Kosher salt

Heat the oil in a large saucepan with a tight-fitting lid over medium heat. Add 5 corn kernels and wait until they pop, about 5 minutes. Add the remaining kernels and cover tightly. Shake the saucepan gently until you hear popping sounds. Stop shaking the saucepan and allow the kernels to pop. Once they have slowed to 2 to 3 pops at a time, about 3 minutes, remove from the heat. Pour into a large bowl and toss with the butter. Add the cheeses and pepper and season with salt. Toss to combine.

Cast-Iron Cookie Sundae

Normal cookies are great. Giant cookies are better, as anyone who's ever been on the receiving end of a cookie cake will attest. This cast-iron skillet cookie takes all the rolling and scooping out of cookie-baking, letting you go from zero to cookie that much faster.

You can also use this recipe to make a half batch of regular-sized cookies, or double the measurements here for a full batch. Just divide the dough into 6 balls and drop onto an unlined baking sheet. Refrigerate for 2 hours, then bake at 350°F for 15 minutes. And if you want to get really innovative here, use those cookies to make ice cream sandwiches for another movie night snack.

SERVES 4

For the COOKIE
1 cup all-purpose flour
¼ cup cocoa powder
1½ teaspoons kosher salt
½ teaspoon baking soda
½ cup unsalted butter, at room temperature, plus more for greasing
½ cup granulated sugar
½ cup packed light brown sugar
1 large egg
½ teaspoon vanilla extract
½ cup peanut butter chips
½ cup semisweet chocolate chips

For SERVING
Vanilla ice cream
Whipped cream
Chocolate sauce
Sprinkles
Maraschino cherries

Whisk together the flour, cocoa powder, salt, and baking soda in a bowl; set aside. Grease a 9-inch cast-iron skillet and set aside.

In a large bowl, beat the butter and sugars with a hand mixer on medium speed until fluffy, about 3 minutes. Add the egg, beating well until smooth; beat in the vanilla. Add the dry ingredients and beat until just combined, then stir in the peanut butter and chocolate chips. Flatten the cookie dough into the prepared skillet and refrigerate for at least 2 hours.

Heat the oven to 350°F. Bake the cookie until puffed, about 25 minutes. Remove from the oven and let cool slightly in the skillet, then top with ice cream, whipped cream, chocolate sauce, and sprinkles. Oh, and don't forget a cherry.

Taco Night

TACO NIGHT

Don't get us wrong—we love the fact that "Taco Tuesday" gives us a reason to gorge ourselves on tacos at least once a week. But, uh, we also want to eat tacos any time the opportunity presents itself, regardless of whether or not it's under the banner of a snappy catchphrase. Turn your house into the taqueria you wish to see in the world, any night of the week, with this veritable buffet of taco options and a classic, no-frills margarita. And, of course, there also needs to be a luscious caramel flan; this version, baked right on top of a perfectly moist chocolate cake, not only defies what would appear to be the laws of culinary physics but also surpasses our highest dessert expectations. We also recommend repurposing these nachos for any ol' night of Netflix or football watching.

Classic Margarita

Margaritas are always best prepared to order, but if you're entertaining a crowd and pressed for time, save time by mixing up a big pitcher of tequila, Cointreau, and lime juice in the same 2-1-1 ratio that you see in the ingredients, then keep it chilled in the refrigerator until you're ready to serve your guests. Want to be totally hands-off once things get going? Salt the rims of several cocktail glasses and set them out on the bar with extra garnishes for guests to serve themselves at will.

<u>SERVES 1</u>

Kosher salt
Lime wheel
2 ounces tequila
1 ounce Cointreau
1 ounce freshly
    squeezed lime juice

Put the salt in a shallow dish and rub the rim of a cocktail glass with the lime. Dip the rim of the glass in the salt.

Combine the tequila, Cointreau, and lime juice in a cocktail shaker filled with ice. Shake vigorously and strain into the prepared glass. Garnish with the lime wheel.

Tomatillo Salsa

Leftover tomatillo salsa is one of the best things you can have in the house at any time of day. It's excellent on eggs or steak, or simmer tortilla chips in it for ultra-easy chilaquiles that will defeat any hangover (especially topped with a fried egg).

MAKES 2 ½ CUPS

1 pound tomatillos, husks discarded, rinsed
3 serrano chiles, stemmed
2 garlic cloves, peeled
½ medium white onion, roughly chopped
1 cup fresh cilantro leaves and tender stems
Kosher salt

Cover the tomatillos, chiles, garlic, and onion with water in a medium saucepan and bring to a boil. Reduce the heat to maintain a simmer and cook until the tomatillos are soft, about 30 minutes. Strain and cool slightly, then transfer to a blender with the cilantro. Puree until smooth, then season with salt. The salsa will keep, covered and refrigerated, for up to 1 week.

Fried Fish Tacos

By dredging your fish in a wet batter before coating it in seasoned dry flour, you get a flaky, textured, crispy crust while the fish stays moist and juicy. While you're frying, be sure to skim out any bits of batter that are starting to burn and turn black, as those pieces will make all of the oil—and thus your fish—taste bitter.

SERVES 6 TO 8

3 cups thinly sliced red cabbage
½ cup white vinegar
Kosher salt and freshly ground black pepper
1 cup sour cream
Zest of 1 lime, plus 2 tablespoons freshly squeezed juice
2 cups all-purpose flour
2 tablespoons paprika
1½ teaspoons cayenne pepper
1 tablespoons baking powder
1 (12-ounce) can light beer
1 large egg
Vegetable oil, for deep-frying

1½ pounds cod, cut into ¾-inch by 2- to 3-inch long pieces
16 (6-inch) flour tortillas, for serving
2 tablespoons roughly chopped fresh cilantro
Lime wedges, for serving

In a medium bowl, toss the cabbage with the vinegar and season with salt and pepper. Set aside until ready to serve.

Mix the sour cream with the lime zest and juice, then season with salt and pepper. Cover and refrigerate until ready to use.

In a large bowl, whisk together a dry mixture with 1 tablespoon salt, 2 teaspoons black pepper, the flour, paprika, cayenne, and baking powder. Make a wet batter by transferring half of the dry ingredients to a separate bowl and whisking in 1 cup of the beer and the egg (drink the rest of the beer!).

Heat 2 inches of vegetable oil in a large saucepan until a deep-fry thermometer reaches 350°F. Line a plate with paper towels. Working with one piece of fish at a time (and using one hand

continued

Fried Fish Tacos continued

to hold wet ingredients and the other for dry), dip the fish in the wet batter, then in the dry mixture. Fry the fish until crispy and golden, about 2½ minutes. Using a slotted spoon or spider (page 9), transfer to the paper towel–lined plate and season with salt. Repeat with the remaining fish.

Meanwhile, heat the tortillas up either directly on the flames of your gas stove or in a cast-iron skillet over high heat, using tongs to flip them, until lightly charred. Place 2 or 3 pieces of fish in the middle of each tortilla, then top with the cabbage, sour cream mixture, and cilantro. Serve with lime wedges on the side.

On Tortillas

Lots of people will tell you there's only one kind of tortilla for tacos. Those people are wrong. The best tortilla for a taco is the one you feel like eating; we like flour for these fish tacos because they hold up nicely to an onslaught of fillings. If you have corn at home, make these with corn (double up if you have to, so that the fish doesn't fall through). Crispy taco shells tend to do best with non-crispy fillings (just so that there's some textural difference in the dish), but honestly . . . there's no such thing as a bad taco.

Ground Beef Tacos

Look, we know hard-shell tacos get a bum rap, but there's something gnarly-good and nostalgic about those crispy corn tortillas. If you feel like your pride takes a hit from using store-bought hard-shell tacos, take comfort in knowing you're making your own spice mix for the beef, and not stooping quite so low as to use those seasoning packets from the grocery store condiment aisle.

18 hard taco shells
2 tablespoons cornstarch
1 tablespoon garlic salt
1 tablespoon ground cumin
1 tablespoon onion powder
1 tablespoon paprika
2 teaspoons cayenne pepper
2 teaspoons ground coriander
3 tablespoons vegetable oil
2½ pounds ground beef

Kosher salt and freshly ground black pepper
8 ounces finely shredded Mexican cheese blend
1½ cups shredded iceberg lettuce (about ½ head)
2 to 3 tomatoes (about 1 pound), finely chopped
8 ounces sour cream

Heat the oven to 375°F. Arrange the taco shells in an even layer on a baking sheet and set aside.

In a medium bowl, combine the cornstarch, garlic salt, cumin, onion powder, paprika, cayenne, and coriander. Heat the oil in a large skillet over medium-high heat. Add the ground beef and cook, breaking up the pieces with the back of a wooden spoon, until browned, 5 to 7 minutes. Add the spice mixture along with 1 cup water and bring to a boil. Cook, uncovered and stirring occasionally, until thick, about 4 minutes. Season with salt and pepper and keep warm.

Meanwhile, heat the taco shells in the oven for 5 minutes.

Divide the meat among the taco shells and top with the cheese, lettuce, tomatoes, and sour cream.

Carnitas

You may not have cooked with lard before—what with living in the age of low-cal everything and "fat is bad" hysteria—but there are some situations when only good ol' fashioned rendered pork fat will do. When you crank the heat to crisp the meat right before serving, you're going to want a fat that can handle it without smoking. Trust the lard. (But if you have trust issues, go with vegetable oil instead.) You can make this through the first step up to three days in advance.

SERVES 6 TO 8

6 tablespoons lard or vegetable oil

2 pounds boneless, skinless, pork shoulder or butt, cut into 3-inch pieces

Kosher salt

6 garlic cloves, peeled and smashed

3 Pickled Jalapeños (page 23), roughly chopped, plus 2 tablespoons pickling liquid

1 large white onion, diced

½ cup whole milk

2 limes, halved, plus ½ cup freshly squeezed juice

2 oranges, halved, plus 1 cup freshly squeezed juice and wedges, for serving

½ cup chopped fresh cilantro leaves

Corn tortillas, for serving

Tomatillo Salsa (see page 134), for serving

Melt 4 tablespoons of the lard in a large saucepan over medium-high heat. Season the pork all over with salt, then cook, turning as needed, until browned all over, 12 minutes. Add the garlic, jalapeños and pickling liquid, and half of the onion. Squeeze the limes and oranges into the pan and chuck the spent halves in there. Top with the milk and the lime and orange juices. Bring to a low simmer, cover, and cook until the pork is really tender, 1½ to 2 hours. Transfer the pork to a cutting board and use two forks to shred the meat. Strain the cooking liquid, discarding the solids, and transfer the pork and the liquid back to the saucepan, stirring to coat. Keep warm.

Heat a large cast-iron skillet over high heat. Melt the remaining 2 tablespoons lard and add as much of the meat to the skillet as will fit in a single layer. Cook, stirring occasionally, until the pork is crispy, 4 minutes. Repeat with the remaining pork, in batches. Divide among the tortillas and top with the remaining chopped onion and cilantro. Serve with salsa and orange wedges.

Loaded Nachos

You don't actually need a recipe to put stuff on chips, but this particular combination of pico de gallo, queso, guacamole, sour cream, crisp radishes, and fresh cilantro is pretty soigné. If you wanted to, you could use whatever shredded cheese you have on hand in place of the liquid queso, but then you actually have to turn the oven on and slide this whole mountain of chips under the broiler and pray that the cheese has time to melt before you turn the tortilla chips into charcoal. That's why we have you make queso.

For the PICO DE GALLO (MAKES ABOUT 2 CUPS)

⅓ cup finely chopped fresh cilantro

2 small tomatoes, cored and diced

½ jalapeño, stemmed, seeded, and finely chopped

½ small white onion, diced

Zest and freshly squeezed juice of 2 limes

Kosher salt and freshly ground black pepper

For the GUACAMOLE (MAKES ABOUT 2½ CUPS)

1 small jalapeño, stemmed, seeded, and finely chopped

1 small tomato, stemmed, seeded, and finely chopped

½ red onion, finely chopped

¼ cup freshly squeezed lime juice

3 tablespoons finely chopped cilantro

3 avocados, peeled, pitted, and finely chopped

Kosher salt and freshly ground black pepper

For the QUESO (MAKES 4 CUPS)

16 ounces shredded Oaxaca cheese (about 1¾ cups)

16 ounces Velveeta cheese, cubed

1 cup whole milk

2 Pickled Jalapeños (see page 23), finely chopped

Kosher salt and freshly ground black pepper

For the NACHOS

2 (13.5-ounce) cans black beans, rinsed and drained

Zest of 2 limes

¼ cup freshly squeezed lime juice

Kosher salt and freshly ground black pepper

1 (16-ounce) bag corn tortilla chips

1 cup fresh cilantro leaves

½ cup sour cream

4 radishes, thinly sliced

3 Pickled Jalapeños (see page 23), thinly sliced

continued

Loaded Nachos continued

Make the PICO DE GALLO: Mix all the ingredients in a medium bowl. Season with salt and pepper and cover. Refrigerate until ready to use. Pico de gallo will keep, refrigerated, for up to 3 days.

Make the GUACAMOLE: In a mortar and pestle, lightly smash the jalapeño, tomato, and red onion. Add the lime juice, cilantro, avocados, salt, and pepper and mix well to combine. Refrigerate until ready to use. Guacamole will keep, refrigerated, with a layer of plastic wrap directly on its surface, for up to 2 days.

Make the QUESO: Heat 1 cup of water in a small saucepan over medium heat. Set a heatproof bowl over the saucepan to form a double boiler. Put the cheeses and milk in the heatproof bowl and allow to melt, stirring often. If the mixture seems too thick, add a bit more milk. Once the cheese has melted, stir in the jalapeños and season with salt and pepper. Keep warm.

Make the NACHOS: Put the black beans in a medium saucepan. Lightly mash them with a potato masher and heat over medium heat, stirring occasionally, until warmed through. Stir in the lime zest and juice and season with salt and pepper.

Layer half of the chips on a baking sheet. Top with half of the beans and half of the queso. Top with the remaining chips, beans, and queso. Top with the guacamole, pico de gallo, cilantro, sour cream, radishes, and pickled jalapeños.

Impossible Flan

What makes this dessert impossible? Well, you're making caramel in a cake pan, then topping that caramel with chocolate cake batter, then pouring a flan mixture on top. The result, after it has baked, cooled, and been flipped out onto a serving platter? You're looking at a cake with completely separate layers, with the flan now resting nicely on top of the chocolate cake. WTF, amirite? Plan ahead: it'll need about 4 hours in the fridge to work its magic.

SERVES 8

For the CARAMEL
Unsalted butter, for greasing
1 cup granulated sugar

For the CAKE
1 cup all-purpose flour
1 cup granulated sugar
½ cup cocoa powder
1 teaspoon baking powder
1 teaspoon baking soda
½ teaspoon kosher salt
¾ cup whole milk
¼ cup vegetable oil
1 teaspoon vanilla extract
1 large egg

For the FLAN
½ teaspoon kosher salt
½ teaspoon vanilla extract
4 large eggs
1 (14-ounce) can sweetened condensed milk
1 (12-ounce) can evaporated milk

Make the CARAMEL: Grease a 9-inch round cake pan with unsalted butter and have ready a large baking or roasting pan into which it can fit. Put the sugar and ½ cup water in a medium skillet over medium heat. Stir gently to dissolve the sugar slightly, then leave it be, but keep an eye on it. It will start to bubble as the water evaporates. Around the 15-minute mark, you will notice it changing color to a light amber. You may need to swirl it a bit if there are dark spots. After 1 or 2 more minutes, it will be done. Pour it into the prepared cake pan. To clean the skillet, simply run warm water over it; the remaining caramel will melt away.

Make the CAKE: Heat the oven to 375°F. In a medium bowl, stir together the flour, sugar, cocoa powder, baking powder, baking soda, and salt. In a separate small bowl, whisk together the milk, oil, vanilla, and egg. Pour the wet ingredients into the dry and, using a hand mixer, beat until smooth, then pour into the prepared pan.

Make the FLAN: Put all of the ingredients into a blender or a bowl and mix until smooth. Carefully pour on top of the cake batter. Yes, it's counterintuitive, but don't worry—this is why it's called "impossible." Put the cake pan in the larger baking dish or roasting pan. Transfer carefully to the oven, then pour water into the larger pan so it comes halfway up the sides of the cake pan. Cover the entire thing loosely with aluminum foil and bake until the cake has puffed up and is cooked through, about 55 minutes. Carefully remove from the oven and remove the foil. Cool at room temperature, then refrigerate for at least 4 hours.

To remove the flan from the pan, carefully run a knife around the edge. Invert a plate over it, then hold them securely together and flip them over. The flan should release. (If it doesn't, be patient; if you greased the pan, it'll come out. Tap firmly around the outer rim of the cake pan, then try lifting again.) Slice and serve.

Pizza Party

PIZZA PARTY

It's a truth universally acknowledged that the most essential, most crowd-pleasing food for any party is pizza (and all things related to pizza). And yeah, it's probably going to be a hit even if you just order a large cheese from the closest crappy chain. But show your friends you care—and prove to yourself that you don't need anyone else to make you happy, not even the delivery guy—by making the king of all foods right in your very own home.

Spinach and Mushroom Calzone

A calzone is basically just a giant, finger-food ravioli with pizza dough in place of the pasta. So it makes sense that the filling here is the same as in our ravioli (see page 38). It's also the same as that of our Spinach and Mushrom Lasagna (page 45), because you basically can't go wrong eating carbs with cheese. Oh, and—surprise! The dough is the same one you'll use to make pizza (see page 157).

But you don't have to use this exact filling if you don't want to. What do you like in your calzone? Sausage? Cook Italian sausage out of the casing in a skillet ahead of time and fold it into the rest of the filling before you stuff your dough. Pepperoni? Layer slices on the flattened dough balls before adding the cheese mix. Hate mushrooms? Leave 'em out! And maybe add some peppers in their place. The point is: this is all about the technique, not about bossing you around when it comes to the toppings.

MAKES
2 CALZONES

For the FILLING
2 tablespoons olive oil
1 garlic clove, minced
1 small yellow onion, thinly sliced
Kosher salt
1 pound cremini mushrooms, thinly sliced
10 ounces frozen spinach, defrosted, drained thoroughly, and roughly chopped
1 cup ricotta cheese
1 cup shredded mozzarella cheese
Freshly ground black pepper

For the DOUGH
2¼ teaspoons active dry yeast
½ teaspoon granulated sugar
2 cups all-purpose flour, plus more for dusting
½ teaspoon kosher salt
2 tablespoons olive oil

1 to 2 cups Tomato Sauce (see page 35), for serving

Make the FILLING: Heat the oil in a large skillet over medium-high heat. Add the garlic and onion and season with salt. Cook until soft, about 2 minutes. Add the mushrooms and cook until soft, about 5 minutes more. Add the spinach and cook, stirring, until well blended, 2 minutes more. Transfer the vegetables to a colander to drain for 20 minutes, then press out any remaining liquid from the vegetables. Transfer the vegetables to a bowl, stir in the ricotta and mozzarella, and season with salt and pepper. Cover and refrigerate until ready to use.

continued

Make the DOUGH: In the bowl of a stand mixer fitted with a dough hook, combine the yeast, sugar, and ¾ cup water heated to 115°F (if you don't have a thermometer, you want it to feel hot to the touch, but you should also just get a thermometer). Let sit until foamy, about 10 minutes. Add the flour and salt and mix on medium speed until a smooth dough forms, about 5 minutes. Cover the bowl with plastic wrap and let rise for 30 minutes.

Heat the oven to 425°F. Lightly flour a work surface and line a baking sheet with parchment paper. Divide the dough into two equal-sized balls. On the floured surface, working with one ball of dough at a time, roll the dough out into a 10-inch circle. Transfer the dough to the baking sheet. Spread half of the filling on half of the circle, leaving a ½-inch border. Fold the other half of the dough over the filling and use a fork to seal the edges closed. Brush the oil over the top and cut a few 1-inch slits in the top of the calzone. Repeat with the remaining ball of dough. Bake the calzones until golden, 25 minutes.

While the calzones are baking, heat up the tomato sauce in a small saucepan over medium-low heat, stirring occasionally. Cool the calzones slightly before serving with the tomato sauce.

Grandma-Style Homemade Pizza

We told you the calzone (page 153) dough would come back for the pizza party's pièce de résistance: the pie around which the whole shebang happens. Believe it or not, you don't need a custom-built, wood-fired, million-degree oven—or even a ceramic pizza stone—to make good pizza. This is a grandma-style pizza, which means all you actually need is a baking sheet. (If you don't have a baking sheet, you can use a casserole dish, but you should get a baking sheet.)

As far as toppings are concerned, we think the sauce-and-cheese combo is a classic for a reason, but feel free to treat this as a jumping-off point. Plus, part of what's so cool about mastering the art of homemade pizza is being able to customize the topping situation to exactly what you want.

MAKES 1 (9 BY 13-INCH) PIZZA

For the DOUGH
2¼ teaspoons active dry yeast
½ teaspoon granulated sugar
2 cups all-purpose flour, plus more for dusting
½ teaspoon kosher salt
2 tablespoons olive oil

For the TOPPINGS
½ cup Tomato Sauce (see page 35)
1½ cups shredded mozzarella cheese
Fresh basil leaves
Dried oregano, for serving
Freshly grated Parmesan cheese, for serving
Red pepper flakes, for serving

Make the DOUGH: In the bowl of a stand mixer fitted with a dough hook, combine the yeast, sugar, and ¾ cup water heated to 115°F (if you don't have a thermometer, it should feel hot to the touch). Let sit until foamy, about 10 minutes. Add the flour and salt and mix on medium speed until a smooth dough forms, about 5 minutes. Cover the bowl with plastic wrap and let rise for 30 minutes.

Drizzle the oil onto a 9 by 13-inch baking sheet. Flatten the ball of dough using the palm of your hand and transfer it to the prepared pan. Using your fingers, spread the dough to the pan edges. Cover it with plastic wrap and refrigerate for 20 minutes.

continued

Grandma-Style Homemade Pizza continued

Heat the oven to 425°F. Using your fingers, spread the dough to the edges of the sheet pan once again. Spread the sauce all over the top of the dough, then top with the mozzarella, right to the edges. Bake until the cheese is bubbling and the crust is lightly golden, about 15 minutes. Cool slightly, then sprinkle the fresh basil on top. Serve with oregano, Parmesan cheese, and red pepper flakes.

Pizza Toppings

There are a million ways to top pizza, but one of the cardinal rules can be a little counterintuitive: less is more. Using a gentler hand with the sauce and cheese lets your crust cook through without getting soggy.

There are a few pizza toppings that benefit from precooking: pizzas cook fast, and there's no way you're going to get meat cooked through before the crust is perfect.

Precook raw meats (like bacon, sausage, and meatballs) and heartier veggies (blanch kale or broccoli rabe first; roast most squashes; saute mushrooms with a pinch of salt); and you can go either way on onions (pre-cooking them means they get a little sweeter and less oniony); if you'd rather eat them raw, then slice razor-thin. No need to precook cured meats like salami and pepperoni; they can go on the top of the pizza as-is.

Garlic Bread

The key to making this garlic bread more than just garlic spread on bread is to first make a spreadable paste that'll sink into all the bread's nooks and crannies. This paste-making method comes in handy for all kinds of cooking endeavors, like salad dressing (see page 29), guacamole (see page 143), or anywhere that you don't want to be biting into chunks of garlic, so we suggest treating this garlic bread as a training exercise. No one is going to object to your taking the time to master garlic bread.

To make the paste, chop the garlic finely and push it all into a little pile near the edge of your cutting board. Next, sprinkle kosher salt on the garlic pile. Then just mush the side of your knife blade back and forth over the mixture until it turns into a smooth, pungent paste that can be easily blended into the softened butter.

SERVES 6 TO 8

1 loaf ciabatta, halved lengthwise
½ cup unsalted butter, at room temperature
4 garlic cloves, mashed into a paste
Kosher salt
¼ cup freshly grated Parmesan cheese
1 teaspoon finely chopped fresh parsley
1 teaspoon finely chopped fresh oregano

Heat the oven to 375°F and line a baking sheet with aluminum foil. Put the bread halves, cut side up, on the baking sheet. In a medium bowl, mix the butter with the garlic and season with salt. Spread it in an even layer on the cut sides of both bread halves. Bake until golden and crispy, about 30 minutes. Remove from the oven and sprinkle the cheese and herbs over the top. Slice each half crosswise into 2-inch slices. Serve immediately.

Chopped Salad with Olives and Chickpeas

This salad is not just an obligatory thing to go alongside all that cheese and bread. You legitimately need a crisp, crunchy, acidic mix of fresh flavors here to make this menu feel like an intentional dinner party and not just a late-night study session. That said, there's yet more cheese in this salad, because cheese is valuable and good. This particular salad takes the whole genre beyond soggy leaves and into something that's also quite enjoyable as a meal all on its own. In fact, if you keep some of it undressed, it'll make a great lunch come Monday.

SERVES 6

¼ cup red wine vinegar
6 tablespoons olive oil
1 teaspoon dried oregano
Kosher salt and freshly ground black pepper
8 ounces red cabbage, thinly sliced
3 ounces pitted Castelvetrano olives, smashed by hand
¼ cup sliced almonds, toasted
3 tablespoons freshly grated Parmesan cheese
20 cherry tomatoes, halved

1 small bunch tender kale (like lacinato/ Tuscan), stems removed and discarded, leaves thinly sliced
½ head iceberg lettuce, cored and thinly sliced
½ head radicchio, cored and thinly sliced
1 (15.5-ounce) can chickpeas, rinsed and drained

In a small bowl, whisk together the vinegar, olive oil, oregano, salt, and pepper. Add the remaining ingredients and toss to combine. Serve immediately.

Nutella and Bourbon Tiramisu

Tiramisu is an impressive, old-school Italian dessert that will make your guests feel like they're eating at a dimly lit restaurant with disconcerting ties to the Mafia. You know, in a good way. This is not a traditional tiramisu in the slightest; to be honest, if you served any Italian grandma this tiramisu, she'd side-eye you pretty hard . . . until she tasted it.

SERVES 6 TO 8

2½ cups heavy cream

1 cup mascarpone

¼ cup confectioners' sugar

2 teaspoons vanilla extract

¾ cup Nutella

1 cup whole milk

½ cup packed light brown sugar

2 tablespoons cornstarch

2 egg yolks

2 tablespoons unsalted butter

Pinch of kosher salt

1 (11-ounce) box Nilla wafers

1 cup strong black coffee (not espresso)

2 tablespoons bourbon

1 teaspoon amaretto or ¼ teaspoon almond extract

Cocoa powder, to finish

In a large bowl, whip 2 cups of the cream, the mascarpone, confectioners' sugar, and 1 teaspoon of the vanilla until stiff peaks form.

Put the Nutella in a medium bowl. In a small saucepan, combine the remaining ½ cup cream with the milk, brown sugar, cornstarch, and egg yolks over medium heat. Cook, stirring constantly, until thick, about 5 minutes. Remove from the heat and stir in the remaining 1 teaspoon vanilla, the butter, and the salt. Pour the mixture over the Nutella, whisking, until slightly smooth. Cool slightly, then beat in half of the whipped cream until smooth.

Combine the coffee, bourbon, and amaretto in a bowl. Grab a 4-quart glass bowl, a 9 by 13-inch glass pan or individual glasses. Basically, you're gonna be dipping the Nilla wafers in the coffee mixture and topping it with a layer of the Nutella mousse and the whipped cream. And then you just keep on layering until you've used everything, ending with a layer of cream. Sieve some cocoa powder over the top and serve immediately.

Easy Grilling

EASY GRILLING

Here's a little secret: grilling outdoors is easy. Or at least, it's not any harder than the cooking you do inside. The whole flame situation may seem intimidating, but if cavemen could do it, so can you (that's not a universal sentiment; please don't try to chase down your dinner with sharpened sticks). It's the best way to combine cooking with being outside, and it's the only way to get that true charred flavor.

Grilled Corn with Feta and Sumac

All grilled corn really needs is a little butter—if that—to be the perfect accompaniment to whatever protein situation you're planning. But don't let it be the unsqueaky wheel that never gets the grease; expect more from your corn and help it deliver by taking the seasoning seriously. See the frittata recipe on page 96 for more on sumac—we think it's essential here.

SERVES 4 TO 8

½ cup Greek yogurt
2 tablespoons freshly squeezed lemon juice
Kosher salt and freshly ground black pepper
4 ears corn, shucked

¾ cup crumbled feta cheese
1 tablespoon finely chopped fresh mint
1 tablespoon finely chopped fresh parsley
1 teaspoon sumac

In a medium bowl, mix the yogurt with the lemon juice, salt, and pepper. Cover and refrigerate until ready to use.

Make a fire in a charcoal grill or preheat a gas grill to medium-high heat. Grill the corn, turning as needed, until the kernels are tender and charred, about 15 minutes. Transfer to a platter. Smear each ear of corn with some of the yogurt, then sprinkle with the feta, herbs, and sumac.

Grilled Caesar Salad

Caesar salad is great; grilled Caesar salad is better. Grilling the leaves adds a smoky complexity and wilting the leaves adds a little textural interest. Homemade Caesar dressing is savory and unctuous and so unlike the bottled stuff that reeks of sad desk salads. And, yes, you really do need to add anchovies to the dressing—it won't make your salad taste like fish, it just gives the final product a sort of unplaceable umami flavor. Use the same garlic paste technique we talked about in the garlic bread recipe (see page 160) to ensure that you're not accidentally chomping into a chunk of raw garlic—and don't skimp on the grated Parm.

SERVES 4

8 ounces Italian bread, sliced into 1-inch thick pieces
6 tablespoons olive oil
Kosher salt
4 whole romaine lettuce heads, halved lengthwise
½ cup Caesar Dressing (page 29)

A shitload of freshly grated Parmesan cheese, for serving
Freshly ground black pepper

Make a fire in a charcoal grill or preheat a gas grill to medium-high heat. Brush the bread with 4 tablespoons of the olive oil and sprinkle with salt. Drizzle the lettuce with the remaining 2 tablespoons of oil. Add the bread to the grill and grill, turning occasionally, until charred all over, 6 minutes. Transfer to a large platter to cool slightly, then tear the slices into 1-inch pieces.

Grill the lettuce, cut side down, until charred, about 2 minutes. Flip and char for another 2 minutes, then transfer to a platter with the croutons. Drizzle with the dressing and sprinkle with Parmesan cheese. Grind on some black pepper and grate on a lot of Parmesan cheese before serving.

Pasta Salad with Feta and Olives

This is not the goopy, mayo-drenched pasta salad of yore. And that's no shade on Hellmann's or even Homemade Mayo (page 24), both of which have their time and place. But, crucially, there's nothing in here that will get gross after an hour sitting outside on a patio table or picnic blanket. This is a pasta salad that you can make ahead and forget about, so you can focus on not burning the burgers when it's actually grill time.

SERVES 6 TO 8

8 ounces orzo pasta
6 ounces crumbled feta
1 cup roughly chopped pitted kalamata olives
⅓ cup finely chopped fresh parsley
¼ cup olive oil
Zest of 2 lemons, plus 3 tablespoons freshly squeezed lemon juice

2 shallots, peeled and finely chopped
1 English cucumber, quartered lengthwise and cut into ½-inch pieces
Kosher salt and freshly ground black pepper

Bring a large pot of generously salted water to a boil. Add the orzo and cook, stirring occasionally, until al dente, about 9 minutes. Drain, then run under cold water until cold. Drain again and dry slightly, then transfer to a bowl with the remaining ingredients. Season with salt and pepper.

Beer Can Chicken

What's great about beer can chicken is that you get to stick a beer can up a chicken's . . . cavern, giggle about how silly it looks, and make some excellent food at the same time. This technique feels advanced and innovative, but it's really just making the whole process more foolproof. Grilled chicken can frequently be a little dry, but the alcohol here helps keep the meat moist, while the vertical roast lets the skin crisp evenly all over for the best of both worlds.

SERVES 4

For the DRY RUB
2 tablespoons coarse sea salt
2 tablespoons freshly ground black pepper
1 tablespoon cayenne pepper
1 tablespoon garlic powder
1 tablespoon light brown sugar
1 tablespoon sweet paprika

For the CHICKEN
1 (3- to 4-pound) whole chicken
1 can cheap domestic beer (or a 6-pack: 1 beer for the chicken, 5 for drinking)

Make the DRY RUB: Mix all the ingredients together and set aside.

Prepare the CHICKEN: Pat the chicken dry, and rub the chicken, inside and out, with the dry rub. Slide your fingers between the skin and the meat and get a little bit of rub up in there, too, while you're at it.

Heat a grill for indirect grilling: bank the coals onto one side of the grill once they're lit so that there's a hot part and a cool part. Put a drip pan on the cold side. Pour half of the beer into the drip pan and insert the can with the remaining beer into the chicken so it sits with legs down and wings up. Tuck the wing tips back to prevent excessive burning. Put the chicken on the cooking grate, over the drip pan, using the beer and the ends of the legs to form a tripod. Cover the grill, and cook, rotating the chicken every 15 to 20 minutes, for 1 to 1½ hours, or until the internal temperature reaches 165°F. Transfer the chicken to a cutting board and let rest for about 10 minutes before carving.

Classic Cheeseburgers

Mixing yellow mustard right into the ground meat for these burgers gives them a familiar tangy flavor that you might recognize if you live near an In-N-Out, but it'll also make the mixture looser. Be careful not to overwork the meat—form patties gently and slide them into the fridge for half an hour to set up. This will give the flavors a chance to meld and helps the meat stay together, whether you're cooking the burgers on the grill outside or in a skillet.

MAKES 6 BURGERS

2 pounds ground beef
6 tablespoons yellow mustard, plus more for serving
2 ½ teaspoons kosher salt
12 slices American cheese (about 12 ounces)
2 tablespoons vegetable oil (optional)
6 potato buns, sliced in half
4 tablespoons unsalted butter, at room temperature

Sliced pickles, for serving
Shredded iceberg lettuce, for serving
2 tomatoes, thinly sliced, for serving
Homemade Mayonnaise (see page 24), for serving

Line a baking sheet with parchment paper. In a large bowl, toss the ground beef with the mustard and salt. Form the meat into 6 patties and transfer to the prepared baking sheet. Refrigerate for at least 30 minutes.

If grilling outside: Make a fire in a charcoal grill or heat a gas grill to medium-high heat. Grill the burgers for about 3 minutes. Flip, then top each with 2 slices of cheese. Grill an additional 3 minutes, or until cheese is melted.

If cooking inside: Heat a large cast-iron skillet over medium-high heat until it smokes. Add the oil and the burgers and cook for 2½ minutes. Flip, then top each with 2 slices of cheese. Add a splash of water to the pan, cover, and cook 1½ minutes more. Uncover, then cook 1 more minute.

Brush the inside of the buns with the softened butter. Grill or broil until charred, about 1 minute. Assemble with your favorite toppings and enjoy.

Fruit Crumble

There are legitimate differences among cobblers, crumbles, and their more esoterically named peers (like the buckle, the grunt, and the slump)—but fundamentally, what you need to know here is that the genre is without question the best way to eat fruit. The topping recipe calls for slightly more than you'll need to make one batch of crumble; save the rest in the freezer to top a skilletful of fruit on a later occasion.

SERVES 6 TO 8

1½ cups all-purpose flour
¾ cup granulated sugar
⅓ cup packed light brown sugar
10 tablespoons cold unsalted butter, diced
3 teaspoons kosher salt

2 pounds strawberries, stemmed, and quartered or halved (depending on how big they are)
1 pound blueberries
1 pound raspberries
Vanilla ice cream, for serving

In a medium bowl, toss the flour, ¼ cup of the granulated sugar, the brown sugar, butter, and 2 teaspoons of the salt. Use your fingers to break up the mixture into pea-sized crumbles. Keep them refrigerated until ready to use.

Heat the oven to 375°F.

In a medium saucepan, mix the remaining ½ cup sugar and 1 teaspoon salt with the fruit. Turn the heat to medium and cook, stirring occasionally, until thick, 50 to 55 minutes. Transfer to a 7 by 11-inch baking dish or 9-inch cake pan and top with about two-thirds of the crumbs. (Freeze the remainder for a later crumble.)

Bake until the crumbs are golden and the berries are bubbling, about 1 hour. Cool slightly, then serve hot with the ice cream.

Steakhouse Dinner

STEAK-HOUSE DINNER

When it comes to making you feel like a baller, there's nothing quite like a fat slab of juicy meat paired with a stiff drink and surrounded by an assortment of fancy old-school sides. Usually, this means paying for valet parking, dragging your too-small "nice" shoes out of the back of the closet, and dropping half your paycheck for an old guy in a bowtie to make you steak au poivre tableside. Pro tip: serve up a steakhouse menu at home instead, and you'll make your dining companions feel like a million bucks even if you're just wearing sweatpants.

Once you know how to nail a proper steak (page 53), the rest is a snap. It's not a bad life skill to know how to shake up (or stir) a perfect martini, and a crisp wedge salad and elegantly presented shrimp cocktail might just be two of the easiest ways to make a big impression in a short time frame. And, of course, no steakhouse meal is complete without a generous dollop of creamed spinach. And for dessert? Baked Alaska, with a twist that nods to the Don Draper generation while being anything but a cliché. This dinner will make you feel like you're in a Sinatra song, with or without a white tablecloth.

Classic Martini

There's a reason why the martini hasn't changed much, if at all, in about a century: you can't improve on perfection. Whether you're pro-gin all the way or on Team Vodka, there's little not to love about the wildly simple combination of your spirit of choice, a bit of vermouth, and an easy garnish. Our best advice? Enjoy ice-ice-cold, baby.

SERVES 1

3 ounces gin or vodka
½ ounce dry vermouth
Lemon twist or olives,
for garnish

Pour the gin or vodka and vermouth into a cocktail shaker filled with ice. Either shake or stir it, then strain it into a chilled martini glass. If using a lemon twist as the garnish, gently squeeze the oil from the peel into the glass before dropping the twist in. If going for olives, add them to a skewer and gently slide it into the glass. If you like it dirty, add a splash of olive juice to the cocktail shaker before you shake or stir the drink.

Ultra-Rich Creamed Spinach

There are a million ways to make creamed spinach, but you've never tried this one. Talk about lowbrow meeting highbrow: The two secret ingredients in our take on the traditional steakhouse side are Velveeta and Pernod. Your guests will never guess, but they'll definitely ask for seconds. (Also, this is basically spinach-artichoke dip without the artichokes, so try serving this on its own as a cold-weather, sweatpants-friendly appetizer with bread or pita chips for dipping.)

SERVES 6

3 tablespoons unsalted butter

3 medium shallots, peeled and thinly sliced

2 (10-ounce) packages frozen spinach, defrosted and drained

2 tablespoons Pernod

8 ounces cream cheese, cubed

8 ounces Velveeta, cubed

Kosher salt and freshly ground black pepper

⅛ teaspoon freshly ground nutmeg

Melt the butter in a large saucepan over medium heat. Add the shallots and cook until soft, about 5 minutes. Add the spinach and cook until heated through, about 5 minutes. Transfer the spinach and shallots to a colander and drain the liquid from the pan. Squeeze the liquid from the spinach mixture, too, then return to the pan. Stir in the Pernod and cook until it evaporates, about 2 minutes.

Stir in the cream cheese and Velveeta and cook until the cheese has melted and the mixture is thick, 5 minutes. Season with salt and pepper and add the nutmeg. Serve immediately.

Shrimp Cocktail

If you ask us, the shrimp cocktail should be the first thing on the table (besides your martini) when sitting down to a steakhouse-style dinner. These pink, juicy babies are hit with lemon and pepper and dropped into an ice bath for extra crispness before making their way onto a bed of lettuce, and then, after a bath in some spicy cocktail sauce, straight into your mouth.

SERVES 6

10 whole black
    peppercorns
1 lemon, halved
3 dozen peeled and
    deveined shrimp
Crushed ice
Cocktail Sauce
    (see page 33),
    for serving
Saltines, for serving
Lemon wedges, for
    serving

Bring 6 cups water to a boil over high heat along with the peppercorns and lemon. Reduce the heat to maintain a simmer and cook for 10 minutes. Add the shrimp and cook until the shrimp are pink and firm, 5 minutes. Strain and transfer the shrimp to an ice bath until cold. Drain, then pat dry.

To serve, line cocktail glasses or a platter with the crushed ice and arrange the shrimp on top. Serve with saltines and a bowl of cocktail sauce for dipping. Don't forget the lemon wedges!

How to Crush Ice

Serving shrimp (or oysters or clams on the half-shell) on a bed of crushed ice keeps them juicy and cold, just the way you want them. If you don't have a fridge that delivers crushed ice at the push of a button, wrap regular ice cubes in a clean kitchen towel and use a rolling pin or meat mallet (or heavy skillet) to crush till they're the right consistency.

Wedge Salad with Bacon and Pickled Vegetables

Wedge salad might not sound all that magical at a glance (iceberg lettuce? cherry tomatoes?), but it packs a salty, smoky, creamy flavor punch that to know is to love. Ours is made with thick-cut bacon and an extra-rich dressing, because salad doesn't always need to feel that healthy—especially when it's riding shotgun to a fat steak. Also, pickled radishes and onions help cut the richness of the cheese dressing, just a bit.

SERVES 4

6 radishes, thinly sliced into circles

1 small red onion, thinly sliced

1 cup white vinegar

¼ cup granulated sugar

1 tablespoon kosher salt, plus more to taste

12 ounces thick-cut bacon, sliced crosswise into ½-inch-thick lardons

1 head iceberg lettuce, quartered

1 cup Blue Cheese Dressing (see page 27)

1 pint cherry tomatoes, halved

Freshly ground black pepper

Put the radishes and onion in two small separate bowls. Bring the vinegar, sugar, salt, and 1 cup water to a boil in a medium saucepan. When the sugar and salt have dissolved, pour half of the pickling liquid over the radishes and half over the onion. Let stand until cool. Pickled veggies will keep, covered and refrigerated, for up to 2 weeks.

Heat a large cast-iron skillet over medium heat and line a plate with paper towels. Add the bacon and cook until the fat has rendered and the bacon is crisp, about 9 minutes. Using a slotted spoon transfer to the plate to drain. (Save the bacon fat for frying potatoes or eggs another day.)

To serve, divide the lettuce wedges among individual plates and drizzle with the dressing. Top each with some bacon, onion, radishes, and cherry tomatoes. Grind some fresh black pepper over the top and call it a day.

Grasshopper Baked Alaska

If you were born after 1980, chances are slim to none that you were around for the peak popularity of the grasshopper, a minty chocolate dessert drink that lies somewhere between a pint of mint chip and a White Russian on the flavor spectrum. What goes up must come down—and eventually become popular again (either Plato or Kurt Cobain coined this incredibly meaningful and famous phrase; unclear which) and that brings us to the return of the grasshopper . . . as a proper dessert. A very proper dessert, in fact. A baked Alaska is a combination of cake, ice cream, meringue, and fire, in approximately equal proportions. And sure, it requires a little bit of legwork, but we promise that it's well worth it. Your Aunt Diane would go nuts for this—but so will your hesher brother. (And if it's all too much, just make the brownies—bake them in an 8 by 8-inch pan with the same time and temperature, with or without the mint.)

For the BROWNIE
10 tablespoons unsalted butter, plus more for greasing
4 ounces bittersweet chocolate
4 ounces semisweet chocolate
2 large eggs
1 cup granulated sugar
2 teaspoons mint extract
¼ teaspoon kosher salt
1 cup cake flour, sifted

For the BAKED ALASKA
3 pints of your favorite mint chocolate chip ice cream, preferably green, softened slightly

For the MERINGUE
6 large egg whites (see Separating Eggs, page 72)
1 teaspoon cream of tartar
1 cup granulated sugar

Make the BROWNIE: Heat the oven to 400°F. Grease a 9-inch round cake pan with butter and line with parchment paper. Grease the parchment paper and set the pan aside.

Pour enough water into a 4-quart saucepan to reach a depth of 1 inch. Bring to a boil and reduce the heat to maintain a simmer. Combine the butter and chocolates in a medium heatproof bowl that will fit the saucepan as a double boiler and set the bowl over the pan. Cook, stirring, until melted and smooth, about 5 minutes. Remove from the heat and set aside.

continued

Whisk the eggs together in a large bowl. Add the sugar, mint extract, and salt and whisk to combine. Stir in the chocolate mixture and fold in the flour.

Pour the batter into the prepared pan and spread into an even layer. Bake until the brownie forms a thin skin on top but the batter is still slightly gooey in the center, 18 to 20 minutes. Transfer the pan to a rack and cool completely.

Line a 2-quart glass bowl with a couple of layers of plastic wrap. Scoop the ice cream into the bowl, smoothing it flat on top. Cover with plastic wrap and freeze until hard, about 1 hour.

Make the MERINGUE: Pour the egg whites into a large bowl with the cream of tartar. Using a hand mixer, whip the egg whites until foamy, about 2 minutes. Gradually beat in the sugar until the egg whites are glossy and stiff, 2 to 3 minutes more.

Assembling the BAKED ALASKA: Remove the brownie from the cake pan and place on a plate. Invert the bowl of ice cream onto the brownie. (You may need to run a bit of warm water over the bottom of the bowl to help loosen it.) Peel back the plastic wrap and cover the ice cream completely with the meringue. Form peaks using a spoon to swirl the meringue. Using a kitchen blowtorch, brown the meringue all over. Serve immediately. Alternatively, heat the oven to 500°F and bake until golden all over, about 5 minutes.

Why Cake Flour?

Using cake flour—a lower-protein flour milled from softer wheat than regular flour—makes the brownie layer in this Baked Alaska extra-delicate and tender, which in turn means that when you slice it, it doesn't slide around under the layers of meringue and ice cream. If you don't have cake flour, you can use all-purpose flour in the following way: For each cup of cake flour called for, take a cup of AP flour, take two tablespoons of flour out of it, and replace them with two tablespoons of cornstarch, whisking well to combine.

FYI, bread flour, which we don't call for in this book, is a higher-protein flour that absorbs more liquid, resulting in stiffer, heartier doughs; good for things like, well, bread.

Backyard Barbecue

BACKYARD BARBECUE

Some of us are fortunate enough to live in regions with incredible barbecue (shout-out to Texas, the Carolinas, Kansas City, and, uh, the entire South). The rest of us might have to get a little hands-on to get our fix of good ol' 'murican barbecue and all the mouthwatering sides found alongside it. Yes, there are a million ways to do barbecue, so we're not here to get into the regional sniping over who makes the best ribs. Instead, we're just going to hit you with some recipes that are guaranteed to taste great no matter which state flag is flying over your local post office. Spoiler alert: You don't even need a proper BBQ setup to make this killer pulled pork, spicy slaw, perfect potato salad, bacon-studded collard greens, and life-changing lemon chess pie. Yep—you can make all of it in a regular old kitchen. Don't tell the purists; we might have to go into hiding.

Spicy Vinegar Coleslaw

Sometimes simpler is better, and that certainly applies to coleslaw. If your recipe looks like rocket science, you're doing it wrong. Start with some crunchy cabbage, toss it with a couple of fresh herbs, olive oil, and vinegar, give it all some heat with jalapeño and black pepper, and you, my friend, are good to go. Throw it onto a roll with some pork, or dig in with a fork on the side—slaw is mandatory, but you can eat it your way.

SERVES 6 TO 8

¼ cup finely chopped
    fresh cilantro
¼ cup finely chopped
    fresh parsley
¼ cup olive oil
¼ cup white vinegar
1 teaspoon celery seed
1 Pickled Jalapeño
    (see page 23),
    thinly sliced, plus
    2 to 3 tablespoons
    pickling liquid

½ head green cabbage,
    very thinly sliced
Kosher salt and freshly
    ground black
    pepper

Mix all the ingredients together in a large bowl. Season with salt and pepper and serve immediately.

Classic Potato Salad

Your grandma might have, ahem, strong opinions about how potato salad should be made, but may we suggest you give this version a try? It's as traditional as they come—russet potatoes, homemade mayo, a hit of mustard—but with a little extra attention to detail (think diced gherkins and a hint of shallot). Packed for a picnic or scooped onto a tray, it's the perfect creamy accompaniment to round out the big flavors of brisket, pork, or whatever Big Meat is on your plate.

SERVES 6 TO 8

6 large eggs, at room temperature

3 pounds russet potatoes, scrubbed clean and cut into 1-inch pieces

4 ounces gherkins, diced

½ cup Homemade Mayonnaise (see page 24)

⅓ cup finely chopped fresh parsley

2 tablespoons whole-grain mustard

1 small shallot, peeled and finely chopped

Kosher salt and freshly ground black pepper

Bring a medium saucepan of water to a boil. Gently add the eggs and reduce the heat to maintain a simmer. Cook for 10 minutes, then drain and transfer the eggs to an ice bath until cold enough to peel and dice. Set the diced eggs aside in a large bowl.

Put the potatoes in a large saucepan and cover with water. Salt generously and bring to a boil. Reduce the heat to maintain a simmer and cook the potatoes until tender, 10 minutes. Drain and run under cold water to cool. Transfer the potatoes to the bowl with the eggs and add the remaining ingredients. Season with salt and pepper and serve.

Collard Greens with Bacon and Vinegar

Greens? Meh. Greens cooked with loads of bacon and butter? Hell of a lot more interesting. Thick-cut bacon adds a smoky, savory punch to this easy dish, which is a must-have side in any barbecue spread. Traditional greens recipes simmer for hours; this gets you all the flavor in half the time.

SERVES 6

3 pounds collard greens

12 ounces thick-cut bacon, sliced into ¼-inch thick pieces

2 medium yellow onions, finely diced

4 cups chicken or vegetable stock (see page 31)

6 tablespoons apple cider vinegar

6 tablespoons unsalted butter

Kosher salt and freshly ground black pepper

Remove the collard green leaves from the tough stems by folding the two leaf sides together, then grasping firmly and tearing them upward and away from the thick end of the stem. Roll the tender leaves up like a cigar and thinly slice them about ¼ inch thick.

Cook the bacon in a medium saucepan over medium heat until the fat has rendered and the bacon is crispy, about 5 minutes. Add the onions and cook until soft, 2 minutes more. Add the collards and the stock and bring to a simmer. Cook until the stock has evaporated, about 35 minutes. Stir in the vinegar and butter. Season with salt and pepper and keep warm until ready to serve.

Pulled Pork Sandwiches

Here's a great opportunity to track down the best local butcher in your neighborhood, if you haven't done so already. Then saunter up to the counter and ask for butt—a nice big hunk of pork butt, aka shoulder. Believe it or not, doing this is the most difficult part of this recipe. The rest is setting your oven, seasoning your meat, and kicking back for a few hours. Potato rolls are crucial: you'll want a soft and fluffy bread base to soak up all the good-good. Oh, and you'll want to save the extra barbecue sauce—this salty-sweet condiment tastes great on more than just pulled pork.

SERVES 6

1 (3-pound) piece
    boneless and
    skinless pork
    shoulder or butt
Kosher salt
1 cup Barbecue Sauce
    (see page 34)
Potato rolls, for serving

Heat the oven to 300°F. Season the pork all over with salt and put it in a 9 by 13-inch baking dish, fat side up. Cover with aluminum foil and bake until falling apart and incredibly tender, about 3 hours. Remove from the oven and, using two forks, shred the meat.

Combine the barbecue sauce with the shredded meat. Serve on potato rolls.

Lemon Chess Pie

A classic Southern treat, chess pie is as old as America itself. The first known recipes for this sweet, tart dessert date as far back as the seventeenth century, perhaps because its main components—sugar, eggs, butter, and flour—are so easy to acquire. Once you've set the crust, the filling is as dummy-proof as they come: mix, pour, and bake. Then enjoy, and remember that no matter how bad things get, we've probably still made a few upgrades in the last three hundred years—even if this pie didn't need any.

SERVES 8

For the CRUST
1¾ cups all-purpose flour, plus more for dusting
8 tablespoons unsalted butter, cubed and chilled
2 teaspoons granulated sugar
½ teaspoon kosher salt
1 teaspoon apple cider vinegar

For the FILLING
1 cup granulated sugar
1 cup packed light brown sugar
¾ cup freshly squeezed lemon juice
8 tablespoons unsalted butter, melted
2 tablespoons cornmeal
1 tablespoon all-purpose flour
1 teaspoon kosher salt
6 large eggs, lightly beaten

Make the CRUST: Put the flour, butter, granulated sugar, and salt in the bowl of a food processor and pulse until pea-size crumbles form. Add the vinegar and 3 tablespoons ice-cold water and pulse until a dough forms. Transfer to a work surface and knead the dough until smooth, 1 to 2 minutes. Form into a disk, wrap in plastic wrap, and refrigerate for 1 hour.

On a lightly floured work surface, roll the dough into a 12-inch circle. Transfer to a 9-inch pie pan, pressing the dough into the bottom and up the sides, leaving about a 1-inch overhang. Trim off excess dough and crimp the edges. Refrigerate for 30 minutes.

Make the FILLING: Heat the oven to 375°F. Put the chilled pie shell on a baking sheet. In a large bowl, combine all of the ingredients and mix until smooth, then pour the mixture into the pie shell. Bake until the center is just set, 50 to 55 minutes. Transfer the pie to a cooling rack and cool completely before serving.

Acknowledgments

First and foremost, this book wouldn't exist without the tireless work, energy, creativity, and endless capacity for weird jokes of MUNCHIES culinary director Farideh Sadeghin. If you could bottle whatever it is that makes her function and sell it—well, actually, please don't; the world isn't ready. I (Rupa Bhattacharya, editor in chief) did a couple things here and there, but this book shines because of her, as well as the very hard work of a lot of others:

Huge thanks to our publisher, Ten Speed Press, and the dedicated editorial team guiding this project: editor Dervla Kelly, Kim Keller, Serena Sigona, designer Kara Plikaitis, as well as emeritus editor Emily Timberlake. Big thanks as well to the entire staff at Ten Speed, especially Aaron Wehner, Maya Mavjee, Hannah Rahill, Windy Dorresteyn, David Hawk, Daniel Wikey, and Allison Renzulli.

In the MUNCHIES test kitchen, kitchen manager Amanda Catrini kept the groceries coming and the mood cheery, while interns Jovan Ortiz, Thomas Gallagher, Danny Zembroski, Max Taylor, and Bert Goncalves tested, shopped, and always read recipes through from beginning to end before starting to cook.

Major gratitude to Heami Lee, who shot stunning photographs faster than humanly possible without ever complaining about anything at all ever; to Judy Haubert, who cooked like a fiend and held pasta with the utmost patience; and to Steph Yeh, who provided killer props.

Big ups to the wildly supportive MUNCHIES team: publisher John Martin; and on the editorial side, headnote-writing heroes Hilary Pollack, Hannah Keyser, and Danielle Wayda, as well as Bettina Makalintal and Jan Diolola; on the video side, Clifford Endo Gulibert, Ian Stroud, Elana Schulman, Peter Courtien, Ike Rofe, Cole Carbone, Virginia Tadini, and Brad Barrett, plus cofounders Chris Grosso and Lauren Cynamon.

Thank you to our partners at FremantleMedia, especially Jennifer Mullin, Keith Hindle, and Matt Foster.

Thank you so much to our agents at the Gernert Company: Anna Worrall, Chris Parris-Lamb, David Gernert, and Paula Breen.

Props as well to Sue Chan, Sophia Yablon, Nikki Spilka, and the entire Care of Chan team for their continued help and constant good vibes.

Thanks to VICE cofounders Shane Smith and Suroosh Alvi, CEO Nancy Dubuc, James Schwab, Ciel Hunter, and the entire VICE team, especially our hand models: Hannah Keyser, Danielle Kwateng-Clark, Headley Duncan, Rajul Punjabi, Elizabeth Renstrom, Jerry Janvier, Jan Diolola, Anna Iovine, Judy Haubert, Alyza Enriquez, Diane Paik, Cole Carbone, Maeve Nicholson, Trey Smith, Sara David, Ike Rofe, Sarah Burke, Jack Sunnucks, Meredith Balkus, Alex Zaragoza, Kim Kelly, Dan Ozzi, Elana Schulman, Jessica Moran, Roberto Ferdman, Taylor Shaw, and Amanda Catrini.

Index

Published in the United States by Ten Speed Press,
an imprint of the Crown Publishing Group, a division
of Penguin Random House LLC, New York.
www.crownpublishing.com
www.tenspeed.com

Ten Speed Press and the Ten Speed Press colophon are
registered trademarks of Penguin Random House LLC.

Library of Congress Cataloging-in-Publication Data
is on file with the publisher.

Hardcover ISBN: 978-0-399-58012-3
eBook ISBN: 978-0-399-58013-0

Printed in China

Design by Kara Plikaitis

10 9 8 7 6 5 4 3 2 1

First Edition